Senior Housing Marketing

How to Increase Your Occupancy and Stay Full

By Diane Twohy Masson, CASP

Cover and illustrations by Steve Hartley

ISBN: 145642632X
ISBN 9781456426323

Printed in the United States of America.

Table of Contents

Introduction
The 12 Keys to Increasing Occupancy

It's challenging for senior citizens to sell their homes and move into retirement communities. But obviously they are doing it. Do you want them to relocate to your place or your competitor's?

This book was written to help CEOs, CFOs, administrators, and marketing directors determine if their marketing teams are performing optimally with every single marketing encounter. Find out if your marketing team might be sabotaging potential sales. Discover new strategies to develop a strong and consistent occupancy marketing program.

The strategies within this book will also provide your new or current salesperson insight into the senior mindset and how to strategically sell your retirement community.

While many senior living communities have been coasting on robust wait lists for years, in many cities, the days of lists are gone and apartment homes are sitting open. You and your team may be experiencing some challenges in occupancy for the first time. Is it the economy? Your team? Or your strategy? This book will provide you with 12 keys to building occupancy at your retirement community.

Sometimes you need to search for and identify a problem in order to solve it. If you keep doing what you are currently doing, you will end up with the same results. Or worse.

By sharing the 12 keys to unlocking your occupancy blockade, I will help you work toward 100 percent occupancy. In addition to these keys, your success will depend on several factors:

- The quality of your organization
- Your current brand image to your future customers
- The satisfaction of your existing residents
- Realistic pricing in relationship to current home values
- How incentives are utilized in comparison with the competition
- The budget allocated to generate new leads
- Last but not least, the expertise of the marketing team

This book is a culmination of my entire sales life. First, I want to credit my husband, Chris. He was my first sales manager. Secondly, I would like to express gratitude to all the senior housing colleagues I have collaborated with over the years. Finally, I want to acknowledge the hundreds of books and audios that I have utilized to improve myself and keep growing every day. Special thanks go to Kim Kimmy, Kathy and Rick Kroll, Cathy and Leigh Goodrich, Eileen Twohy Wyatt, Stephen Magladry, Joan Reynolds, and Jeannette Acheson for their support of this book.

Enjoy the illustrations by Steve Hartley. They add humor to this business we love and, yes, admit it, obsess over. Our passionate careers are geared toward helping seniors find security, connectivity, joy, and peace of mind.

Boost sales and move-ins immediately with the key tips I've included in every chapter. Using these principles, you can increase your occupancy and stay full!

Looking forward to hearing about your successes after using the strategies in this book,

Diane Twohy Masson

Website: www.marketing2seniors.net
E-mail: diane@marketing2seniors.net
Twitter: @market2seniors

Chapter 1
Attitude toward Occupancy – Turn *Your* Change into Dollars

When you looked in the mirror this morning, what was your reflection... joyful, grumpy, or indifferent? What would it take to rev up your engines and put on a happy glow for your colleagues and customers? Maybe you need that first cup of coffee to turn that frown into a smile.

The attitude of a marketing director can literally increase or decrease your occupancy. Why is so little care given to this key "attitude" component of success? It's a missing ingredient in many organizations. That's why it's featured as an early chapter of this book. **We will explore how marketing directors can keep a positive attitude, even with the pressure of occupancy at their throats.** We will also explore how the attitude of everyone in the community can either generate a positive atmosphere (Optimistic Olivia) or create strife that may affect occupancy (Negative Nellie).

How does your workday begin? See if you recognize yourself in any of these scenarios, whether you live alone or with others:
Do you have a cup of coffee or tea and spend the first few minutes of your day complaining and worrying about your aches and pains,

appearance, car, commute, spouse, neighbors, or kids? What fills your head at the start of the day? Are you watching the negative TV news or reading the "bad news" newspaper?

Or are you sharing positive time with yourself and others in your household? Are you listening to an uplifting motivational CD or radio station, calming or energizing music, or perhaps reflecting on positive affirming quotes?

 **TIP: Your morning activities are opportunities to produce sales—even if it's simply listening to inspirational music on your commute. Use the early part of the day wisely. Consider an educational CD, literature, scripture, or even silence to allow your mind to be meditative and creative. For a list of suggestions, see my website: www.marketing2seniors.net**

It's the struggle of every salesperson to be positive all the time, particularly when engaged with a negative or abrasive customer, either in person or on the phone. Prospects may shout, "I am not interested, don't ever call me again." If you are that salesperson who just got chewed out, you may not feel like it yet, but you must maintain genuine passion and energy in your verbal and nonverbal communications throughout the day.

Residential marketing folks are positive people. We tend to be optimistic and believe the glass is half full. Our personalities make us love to work with people, especially seniors. In a later chapter, you will study personalities and identify each personality type. Salespeople can have any type of personality and still be successful, but you must learn to compensate to relate to different personalities.

As an example, meet the social butterfly sales personality named Social Sam. He must discipline his salesperson mouth to focus on the customer and not just talk about himself. The leader type personality, Strong Sean, will learn to be warm and fuzzy with the social butterfly customer to produce more rapport and, consequently, sales.

Let's look at how fellow staff can support and continually renew each other...

The Attitude of the Executive Administrator/Director

It's a huge challenge to create a completely positive culture within your organization. A positive environment can make all the difference for sales staff. Let's face it: without sales there are no jobs for the rest of the staff, including your own. Happy Hannah personalities can make up 95 percent of your staff, but it only takes one Angry Adam, Pessimistic Peter, Depressed Donna, or Complaining Cathy to slowly poison the culture for all staff.

In staff meetings, take the opportunity to remind staff to genuinely smile at each other during the day, whether they're sitting at a desk or walking down the hall. Create a program of employee recognition for good performance and positive attitudes. This positive culture will create an osmosis effect on the negative personalities. As a result, they begin to absorb "good vibes." Negative Nelson will get to the point where he doesn't feel comfortable venting, because others tune him out. Everyone will develop a bounce in their step if associates lift each other up all the time. Any person can have a bad day, but the positive culture created by the executive administrator will stifle any temporarily negative personalities until they are back to being positive again...hopefully soon! The result may even be immediate because human beings typically run toward pleasure and flee from pain.

An organization's culture is created from the top down. If there is coffee chatter, show up on occasion and ask if anyone has a good new story to share. Your directors and supervisors should be helping you create a positive environment that will lift up the entire team. It is a gift to work in a community that feels like family. Everyone's positive attitude will lift fellow employees and generate feelings of goodwill toward residents. If guests and visitors feel the positive atmosphere the minute they walk in the door, they will want to move in—and stay. Prospects, residents, and staff will feel the positive energy in the building created by the culture you foster.

The Attitude of Executive Management

There's tremendous pressure for your marketing staff to perform and keep occupancy high. Remember, you are their boss. You can and should handle a higher level of stress than is expected of them. Maintain a balance in your communications with them about occupancy goals. It can mean the world to the marketing team if they know you believe in them and trust their capabilities.

In tough economic times, everyone has to do twice the work to get the same results as in a good economy. **It's your job to protect the marketing team from feeling too much pressure—every minute.** Please refer to the next section on the CFO to determine general principles of advertising cost outlays for marketing to be effective.

marketing2seniors.net

The Attitude of the CFO

Be kind and thoughtful to the marketing director and his or her team. They are usually extroverted (Excited Edmund) while you, the CFO, tend to be introverted (Analytical Alexander). Your financial projections are vitally important to the long-term finances of the organization. The marketing staff can't shove the concept of moving to your community down someone's throat. It is necessary to have enough qualified candidates walking in the door. This will take some promotional campaigns and advertising efforts that will be discussed in Chapter 6 on Events and Chapter 12 on Media Buying.

If the marketing people are pounded daily about reaching occupancy numbers, they can be so pressurized that they pass that pressure on to the prospective residents. This approach is similar to that of used car or timeshare salespersons. Once the word of high-pressure sales hits the senior's circle of friends, no one will want the free lunch and tour offered by the community. They know someone will grind on them to move in now.

How can you hit your occupancy numbers?

1. Set Realistic Goals – for the year and on a monthly basis. Invite marketing to have input into these goals.
2. Create an adequate budget to generate walk-ins and new lead sources.
3. Short-Term Goals – Have a marketing report sent to you once a week. Review the goals with the marketing team twice a month or once a month depending on the level of occupancy (NOT EVERY DAY)! A sample report is shown in the next section.

4. Please remember to thank the marketing team for their reports.

CFOs crunch numbers! Marketing folks tend to be word people rather than number lovers. So there can be a clash if the marketing person does not give concrete information to the CFO. Avoid this clash. The CFO and the marketing director should work side by side at least once a month. Many organizations don't operate like this because it would be going over the executive director's head. Either way, marketing reports need to satisfy the CFO and the executive director.

Occupancy-driven Marketing Reports that will Wow Your CFO

As the marketing person who prepares the executive level marketing report, keep asking yourself if it's in a "black and white format." In other words, just state the facts, period. Start with how many move-ins you want and work in reverse order. Figures for reports may come from your database software—such as REPS. See the example outlined below.

Goal: The community wants four move-ins each month

1. The Tour to Move-in Ratio is____?
2. The Calls (leads) to Tour Ratio is____?
   (Include out-going and in-bound calls)
3. Total Number of Leads ____?
4. Total Cost of Advertising ____?
5. The Cost per Lead ____?
   (Cost per lead is the total cost of advertising divided by the number of leads)

These are the kind of "non-grey area" numbers that the CFO and executive director will appreciate from you. Marketing rarely has an unlimited budget to attempt an untested campaign. Those holding the purse strings need their marketing professional to articulate in detail exactly how much new money is needed to increase occupancy and how you're going to achieve it. False promises, probabilities, maybes or what ifs will not be appreciated. If you increase your tour traffic with qualified leads, you will generate the needed move-ins. Marketing is an art form.

Tip to CFOs: Marketers like to make the report sparkle, so read the whole chart from left to right including the words highlighted in blue.

Here's how every marketing director can communicate in black and white with the CFO so everyone's attitude improves.

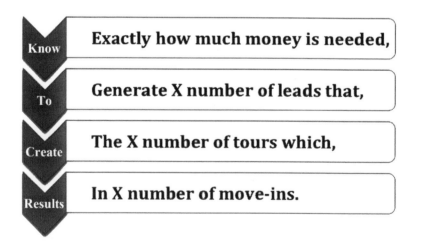

Know — **Exactly how much money is needed,**

To — **Generate X number of leads that,**

Create — **The X number of tours which,**

Results — **In X number of move-ins.**

This is the type of information reporting that a CFO will find most useful. When the marketing director speaks about budget items such as public relations, social media, and community relations, the chief financial officer will listen. Public relations (PR) to create goodwill within your community and town are necessary for long-term benefits. Usually, however, good PR does not have an immediate effect on occupancy. If done properly, good PR *can* have an immediate effect, such as when your community gives tours to city council members and owners of neighboring properties who have an aging loved one. These are key contacts that will create a buzz about your community.

It's all about attitude. I love CFOs. If you learn to love them, they will become your best friends and advocate for a higher marketing budget in tough times. This will increase occupancy. Remember to stick to the facts and have a plan. Give your CFO a report every month. Show how many new leads were generated from advertising. Demonstrate that you are tracking results. Some endeavors will not be successful. This is okay if the CFO understands that you are not just trying to throw mud on a wall to see what sticks. An effective marketer should never throw hard-earned money away just to advertise. There needs to be a comprehensive marketing plan. This will articulate the expenditures necessary to generate the leads that will increase the occupancy.

Do You Live in Fear of the Numbers?

If the targeted occupancy goal is 95 percent and you are running at 90 percent, 85 percent, or less, how *can* you function under this pressure? How can you keep this stressor out of your interactions with the customer? Are you Unbelieving Ursula—wringing your hands and scratching your head? Or are you Believing Betty— charming prospects by painting a pretty picture of their potential lifestyle in your amazing community?

marketing2seniors.net

As a rule, when people are stressed they become cranky, irritable, snappy, easily angered, negative, crabby, and basically not much fun to be around. Why would customers want to go on a tour with a marketer in this stressed-out condition? Why would they want to move into your community? They are trying to de-stress their lives by moving to a retirement community where they have plenty of services and good care. They don't want to hear your problems or experience your negative attitude. They don't want to be sold a place to live; rather, they want to buy peace of mind from living at your community.

The Appointment with Your Customer

The customer should never be made aware of your problems or challenges. I once overheard a salesperson explaining to a potential resident how he had to take his cat to the veterinarian that morning. This poor senior had to listen to all the woes concerning the salesperson's cat. Are you kidding? First of all, why would a marketer interject anything negative into the tour of a fantastic community when the occupancy needs to increase? Secondly, why would a marketer want a prospective resident to be thinking about an ailing cat instead of dreaming of a new life?

Marketers can sabotage possible sales with the wrong approach. This is not about YOU. If your community allows pets, focus on the future resident's pet. Learn the animal's name and then invite the future resident to talk about Fluffo. This is an opportunity to create an emotional connection with him or her.

One hundred percent of the marketing team's focus should be listening to customers and understanding their needs. This information is helpful in customizing your community's features and services to satisfy those needs. There's no greater fulfillment in life than to help other people improve their lives. If you bring this attitude to every appointment, and there are enough people walking through your doors, occupancy will take care of itself. Many marketing people believe their work is more than a job. They consider it a social service or a ministry. These folks are making a difference in the world, building one relationship at a time. Are you this type of marketer?

Your prospective customers will feel your attitude and passion. This alone will intrigue them and keep communication progressing with strength. They know intuitively if you are looking out for their best interests or merely want to fill the building for a commission. Your verbal and nonverbal communication in a customer meeting says it all. If you're listening 100 percent, you don't have time to talk about yourself. Every word that comes out of your mouth will be for the prospective resident's benefit.

Patience is needed. It can take six months to ten years from an initial meeting to a move-in. It's a long-term relationship. Every time you contact the customer, your purpose should be to share some new information—period. It can be a construction update, a new restaurant within walking distance of your community, a fantastic resident outing that you describe in vivid detail, an upcoming community performance that you are inviting them to, the list goes on and on.

People appreciate genuineness. Sadly, it's rare these days for someone to genuinely care. Let them feel your desire to have them understand and appreciate the lifestyle of being a resident. They want to hear more and understand the residential life in your community. This helps them determine that it is the lifestyle they want for themselves. Keep painting the dream...

Gratitude and Fear Can't be in Your Mind at the Same Time

This is one of the greatest statements I have personally learned, especially when the economy hits a significant rough patch. Every morning and every evening, bring to mind five things that you are truly grateful for. Write them down. Dwell on these. In twenty-one days your attitude will be soaring with the eagles. While you are working on an attitude of gratitude, take time to...

...Recharge Yourself

For me, exercising three times a week keeps my stress level to a minimum. It releases endorphins into my body that counteract stress. All work and no play can make anyone dull, boring, and stressed. Here are some ideas:

Learn what recharges you, so you can be at your optimum:

1. **Introverts recharge best by themselves**
2. **Extroverts recharge best with a friend or friends**

Recharging Yourself With Nature and Sports Venues Helps Your Mind Relax!

- Go to a sporting event and shout for your team to win—it really releases stress!
- Bike ride together (babies can be put on the back or pulled in a bike trailer)!
- Walk on the beach and look for seashells.
- Rent canoes and take a picnic lunch.
- Get out on a motorboat (maybe your friend has one and will let you drive?)
- Snow ski or water ski.
- Hike a mountain or trail.
- Go camping.
- Cook s'mores over a campfire.
- Play nine or eighteen holes of golf.
- Join a softball league.
- Play touch football.
- Jump rope.
- Shoot some hoops with a friend or play "pig" or "horse."
- Lap swim.
- Bird watch.
- Swing at a playground.
- Take different routes (from the ones you usually use) when running your errands.

Here are some recharging ideas for extroverts:

- Have a glass of wine or a beer with friends.
- Go to a party.

- Play a game that you enjoy with family or friends.
- Take a vacation with your best friend or family.
- Join a Bible study group.
- Go dancing, sing karaoke, or enjoy music at a club.
- Splurge and go to a concert or play.
- Join a choir.
- Begin yoga or a tai chi class.
- Pull kids in a wagon.

Here are some recharging ideas for introverts:

- Cozy up in front of a fireplace.
- Soothe yourself with music, either at home or driving in the car.
- Learn something new; it gets your creative juices working again.
- Take a bubble bath.
- Watch a movie.
- Read a book (fiction or non-fiction).
- Send greeting cards to old friends, your great-aunt, a shut-in, etc.
- Begin yoga or tai chi at home.
- Enjoy your hobby: photography, motorcycle riding, playing guitar, gardening, crafts, etc.
- Meditate.
- Enjoy contemplative prayer.
- Try strength training or lifting weights.
- If it relaxes you, play on your computer or video games.
- Try scrapbooking—it releases your creativity.
- Pet or groom your animal.
- Do crossword or jigsaw puzzles.

marketing2seniors.net

Let the "No's" Bounce off Your Back

Sales and rejection can go hand in hand. When the customer says yes to being put on the wait list, yes to scheduling an appointment, yes to moving into the community, yes to your hardest apartment to sell, or yes to the most expensive apartment—wow what a feeling! You can ride on that excitement for an hour or a day.

When the customer says no to an appointment, hangs up on you, says something rude on the phone, says he or she decided to move to your competitor (after months of work on your part), says he/she will think about it (after a three-hour appointment), says the kids will not let him or her move in—oh, the let down! Sometimes you just want to wallow in it and go tell the world. Stop it!

- Shake it off and smile and dial the next customer.
- Write "No" on a piece of paper, crumple it up, and throw it away.
- Take a quick five-minute walk to clear your mind.
- Take some deep breaths and picture yourself at the beach (if it helps, go ahead and drown the person that said no in your imagination, so he/she doesn't mess up the view).
- Tell yourself this is why you get paid the big bucks. If everyone could do it, then it would be a minimum wage job.
- Pretend you are a duck and let it slide off your back (sometimes you just need to laugh to break the tension).
- Call someone who is excited about moving in and get recharged!

If you go tell your boss, you will be considered weak, so let it go. Go to the boss only if you notice a pattern of cancellations so that you can strategize how to compete better through the eyes of the customer.

Every Day is a New Opportunity

It's not an accident that we can start over every day. We are all humans and make occasional mistakes. If you hit a rough patch and are pressured by management, shake it off, rethink your attitude, recharge, and get a good night's rest. The next morning is a new beginning! You can make a difference in someone's life today. Your smile or phone call may be the only interaction someone has with a human today. Someone out there could be waiting for your call! Start smiling and dialing; the appointments will come flying in.

If you aspire to greatness, your attitude will follow.

Chapter 2
Quit Blabbing! Control
the Flow of Information

1. **To the Customer and Within Your Organization**
2. **With Resident Referrals**
3. **To Develop a Brand New Community**

What does it mean to control the flow of information to the customer?

It's obvious, right? Don't tell customers information they're not supposed to know. How hard is that? Well, it's not that simple. If you're an executive director and give your marketing director some information that's for him or her to know and the customer not to know—what happens? Unfortunately, it sometimes gets to the customer. This same scenario can take place between a marketing director and his or her staff. Let's talk about it...

A marketing director tells the staff that each one needs to get two sales this month. Period. No excuses. When one of your staff is alone with the prospect at the close of the sale, will he or she tell the customer, "Thank you so much, this is one of my two required sales for the month."? Believe me, it happens. The marketer thinks the customer will be happy for him or her, but it only creates questions in the customer's mind while the customer is heading home.

Controlling the Flow of Information to the Customer and Within Your Organization

Let's begin by going to the top of the organization. Say the CEO or president wants to talk to the executive staff about a confidential matter. At some point the decision is made to pass this information down to middle management and the executive directors of the communities. It might be short-term strategy to counteract the economy or a long-term vision strategy of development. Now it's been determined that marketing directors would benefit from understanding the vision of the corporation so they can strategize how to hit their marketing goals. (I believe that staff members do a better job when they feel they are "in the know" and their roles play a part in the success of the organization.)

Let's face it—some people cannot handle keeping company goals and strategies to themselves and share it with customers. It is usually an innocent act and not done with malicious intent.

So what can you do? I believe it's a case-by-case determination of trust. People within your organization get promoted on your belief in their abilities to be great managers and your level of trust in them. It all comes down to trust. If a strategy is that confidential to the organization, then it must be kept at the highest executive level of management. **People can move into higher management** positions as they prove they can handle absorbing confidential information without sharing it with subordinates. When a strategy is shared with frontline employees, these are the five steps I suggest:

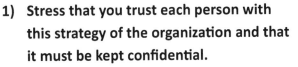

Tip: Five Steps to Controlling the Flow of Information

1) Stress that you trust each person with this strategy of the organization and that it must be kept confidential.

2) Emphasize how the person's role is vitally important to the organization.

3) Share a separate story to be given to the customer that does not explicitly mention the confidential information. (In other words, the customer does not need to get the nitty-gritty details that staff members receive.)

4) Role-play working with a customer/ staff scenario to share only what's appropriate for the customer.

5) Check in the next day (and the next day and the next day) to see how talking to a customer went and to reiterate step number one again.

Please pay attention to this example. It happens more than you can imagine. This could be the very reason your occupancy is down.

Example: The CFOs report stated that the community needs four move-ins per month for the next six months to achieve financial performance and to meet CARF accreditation ratios.

The CFO meets with the executive team to discuss the report, who in turn would talk with the executive administrator.

The executive administrator wants to give the big picture to the marketing director and sales team. They will understand how important CARF accreditation is to the organization.

One assumption here is that no marketer in his or her right mind would say anything about this organizational communication to the customer. Why would anyone even mention financial performance? Salespeople can unknowingly say, "I really need you to move-in within the next six months so our financial performance can meet the CARF accreditation ratios!"

And what would Charlie Brown say to that? "AGHHHHH!"

And what would the prospect's first thought be? "Hmm. This place must not have a good financial performance. People don't want to live here. I don't think I'll move it at all! Next!"

This example does happen! I have personally heard it! You would be amazed to listen in on marketers' conversations and hear how many sales goals are shared with prospective residents. If staff shares inappropriate information, they will not only blow the sale, they will also blow a referral from the sale and so on.

I suggest utilizing "the five steps to controlling the flow of information," including good role-playing exercises between all directors and sales staff. Rehearsals can be practiced during in-service meetings and other staff training events. The entire team will learn what information is for internal use only and which details the customer needs to know to close the sale. Make it fun and over-exaggerate to drive the point home.

Decreasing Apartment Availability

Let's look at another very common scenario. Maybe you have five, ten, fifty, or more apartment homes available. Do you wonder why the number just stays the same and can't be chipped down on a weekly or monthly basis? Realistically you could have a very aged community that has not been updated or you could be over-charging in comparison with the competition. Or it could be that your salespeople are not **creating urgency**.

Let's break this down:

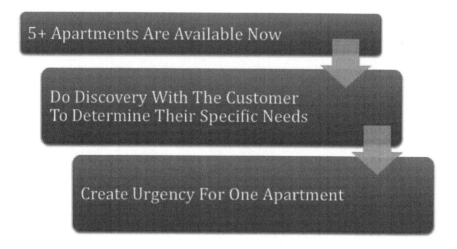

Creating urgency is telling a real story to customers in order to make them want to make a home selection now or they will miss out on the single best apartment home that meets their needs.

Example: My husband and I were checking out a possible dog breed that we were interested in. The goal was to see how that particular breed looked cute as a puppy and as an adult dog. When narrowing down our favorites, I called a breeder and asked if we could view some keeshond puppies. She said absolutely to come and see them. I asked if any were available, and she said that they were all spoken for. I told my husband we were safe from getting a puppy. While we were viewing the puppies, she told us that she was uncomfortable with one of the homes that a potential puppy was going to. We listened intently to her story. Next thing we knew, one of the puppies was going to be ours...

Create Urgency for the Wait List

When prospective residents come to the community for their tour, a salesperson must devote some time to discovering their **immediate** needs. A prospect may be sixty-five years old and ten years away from "needing" (the prospect's word) to move in. Do not oversell to this type of prospect. In your heart, you will know he or she is one major health crisis from moving in. People always consider themselves ten years younger than they really are.

Meet the prospects' current needs, but sell the urgency of the waiting list. For example, "Mr. and Mrs. Smith, I know we have a few openings right now and this is very unusual for us. You said that you are about ten years away. No one can predict the future, and your time line could change (don't say it out loud but you know: either a health event, inability to manage yard work, or the upkeep of a two-level home will shorten their time line). You may be ready in six years and say, okay, Diane, I am ready to move in now. At that time, we may have a two- to three-year wait for an apartment. My suggestion is to make a plan for your future now and get on the wait list. You will keep moving up the wait list, so when you are ready to move in, based on your wait list number, you may be the next person who gets to select an apartment home." Then shut up. If you speak then you immediately lose the sale. They will either choose to get on the wait list or think about it. In the latter case, call them back in one week and talk about how many people are on the wait list, etc., and attempt another close.

Tip: Keep building a relationship with your prospects, following up on the telephone and inviting them to events at your community. I called one prospect once a month for a year before that prospective resident decided to become a wait list depositor. Persistence is a definite key. If you aren't calling, the competition will steal them away.

Residents – Controlling the Flow of Information

Do you have a resident marketing committee? Are some of your residents self-appointed marketing ambassadors? Residents want to help the marketing team increase occupancy. Your residents could unconsciously be sabotaging their own friends from moving in.

Let me give an example:

Norman Applegate says he's on the marketing team and does more than any other resident. He has personally brought in over seventy-five people to tour the community, promotes the community in his annual Christmas card, and invites people to lunch with him at the community. All this work on Norman's part has resulted in zero sales. Why?

If the resident shares absolutely everything and does not encourage the prospect to talk to marketing, then the sale can be lost. Most residents don't realize when their friends are asking buying questions like: "How much are the apartments?" "What is available now?" "How does your health care work?"

If residents give out a price without building value, their friends think it's too much money and reject the idea of living at the community. If the resident gives some kind of bias on the available apartments, this could curtail a sale as well. The marketing staff has the expertise to convey the legally defined health care program and tailor answers to the specific needs of the prospects for their complete understanding of its value and peace of mind.

Tip: Teach the resident marketing committee or resident ambassadors how to respond to their friends' inquiries. What are they supposed to say when a friend asks, "How full are you?" "How much does it cost to live at your community?" "What homes are available now?" Have the residents redirect their friends' questions to the marketing department to give them accurate answers.

Developing a Brand New Community – Controlling the Flow of Information

When you are rolling out a new community, there must be a marketing plan for every month. General marketing goals for a new development are:

- Determining how many families per month to add to the priority group (people who make a deposit and someday want to live there). To have two hundred families in nine months is aggressive, but very possible. Three communities I was a part of developing each reached this goal or exceeded two hundred families dramatically.
- Selecting a target month to transition that group of priority members into 10 percent depositors required by the bank.
- Targeting a date for the banks to approve the financing of the construction bonds (usually 70 percent of the building spoken for with 10 percent deposits, although nowadays banks are demanding even higher numbers).

- Developing methods for retaining depositors and keeping them engaged for several years while the building is under construction.

All these marketing goals need to coincide with the development team, the construction team, and the bankers. The construction team can't suddenly start building a building. The plans must include having an experienced project manager to represent the company and an experienced construction firm that has won the bid for constructing your building. The bankers need to be engaged in the entire process and believe in your team in order to finance the project.

So let's say you are the CEO, the manager in charge of the project, or the marketing director leading the sales team. It's vital that you have a clear understanding of the vision and monthly goals. But what gets said to the customer? How do you make sure the salespeople do not over share? First of all, this could be a $250 million project or more. There is a lot on the line.

Your marketing team is probably brand new because you hired them for this development. I suggest giving your team little tests to see if you can trust them. They may obviously know the current goal is 70 percent–10 percent deposits in the bank in order to start construction. Do not tell them the predicted month or they will most likely tell the customer. I have personally found only a small percentage of marketing people in development that can handle knowing the whole vision but are capable of only sharing a small part with the customer.

Again, no one is being malicious in sharing strategic information. It just seems to pop out of marketing people when some of the depositors keep asking for information again and again and again.

My method of talking to the sales team is with a large basket of balls on the table. It could be a basket of golf balls or decorative balls. Every ball represents one month of priority deposit goals. Then share the *Five Steps to Controlling the Flow of Information* in the earlier part of this chapter. Start with the biggest piece first and say the whole basket is the vision of building the new community. One ball could represent the goal of 70 percent of the building spoken for with 10 percent deposits in the bank to start construction. Skip methods for retention and how they are going to keep the customer engaged. That's on a need-to-know month-by-month basis. Then fast forward to the current month's goal (ball) of starting the priority list of people interested in moving in. Explain how their role is vital and how they will fit into the goal.

For example:

- How many lunch and learns per month?
- What is their role at the lunch and learn?
- Capturing all the contact information and entering it into the database.
- Following up with people if they are not priority members to invite them to another lunch and learn or meet with them one on one.

Do not share a priority list event too far in advance. Only share one or two months of information at a time with your team. If the salespeople tell the customer everything that will happen for the next two years, the customer will get bored and go away. It's about maintaining excitement for the priority members, and when you engage them every month, you have something new to share each time.

Are you giving your marketing team new information on a monthly basis? If you don't have something new to tell prospective residents, that's your fault. There is always something fresh and exciting to say. Help your marketing team by collectively brainstorming new ideas. The enthusiasm generated will be contagious as new information is shared with inquiries, prospective residents, the depositors, wait list and priority members each month. Remind staff frequently that you trust them but to share only appropriate information with the prospective resident.

Chapter 3
Dare to Differentiate Yourself from Your Competition

Keep the Waiting List FULL through Branding

What is Your Reputation?

Your Brand Is the Sum of ALL Stakeholders' Perceptions!

Number one: look around your community with a fresh pair of eyes. What do customers see when they drive up, walk through your main entrance, and walk down the halls to your community spaces? Are there cracks in the cement, worn furniture, a smell, or gouges in the walls? You cannot fill a building when there are severe operational issues or concerns that residents and their families perceive as being unacceptable.

 **Tip: Make a list today of what could be potential deal breakers to your stakeholders and create a plan to correct them as soon as possible.**

A brand is far more than your name and logo. It's how the customer perceives your community or organization (of multiple communities) as superior to the competition.

Here's a fun test:

Go to ten retirement communities within a five-mile radius of your community and obtain each of their brochures. When you study all the brochures, you will find they all have identical themes. Why is that? Even the prospects will think all retirement communities are the same and that it does not matter which one they choose. As a marketing person, this can drive you nuts. You want to shout from the mountaintops, "Our community is the best—move here!" At the end of the day, it's your job to show that your community is truly different.

River's Edge Retirement Living
- Great Food
- Beautiful Apartments
- Security
- Health Services

Spring Wood Senior Living
- Great Food
- Beautiful Apartments
- Security
- Health Services

Bubbling Brook Retirement Community
- Great Food
- Beautiful Apartments
- Security
- Health Services

So how do you make yourself stand out from the rest of the pack and differentiate your organization from your competitors'? You need to create a real brand strategy that speaks to your organization's mission, its core values, and the *emotion* you want to invoke from the public when they see or hear about your brand. Examples of great branding are Nike, Starbucks, Nordstrom, Betty Crocker, or Disney. These well-known brands spent a lot of money to create their brands—but you don't need to. Let's break it down...

The customer makes assumptions about your brand all the time. When residents live in your community and interact with the staff—is the staff exceeding their expectations? How do your resident satisfaction surveys measure against the competition? (You are conducting a satisfaction survey at least once a year—right?) What about when family and friends come to visit the residents? Are they blown away with great service and excellent food and wish that they lived there even though they are not yet old enough? What about guests visiting health services? Do they feel it's institutional and want to get out as soon as possible or is it residential and homey? What do vendors, city officials, and other local businesses think of your organization? Your current reputation is already in the minds of all these stakeholders, so is it good, bad, or just "average"—in other words, no different than the competition?

It's a big decision to create a truly enticing brand strategy that every single person in your organization stands behind. But it is a decision that must be made. There needs to be total branding buy-in from the board of directors, corporate management, executive directors, middle management, marketing directors, sales staff, dining staff, health services staff, maintenance staff, housekeeping staff, concierges, valets, vendors, and administrative support staff. Finally, remember your biggest stakeholders: the current residents and prospects.

From the top of the organization to the frontline staff, every single person needs to know your brand and how the prospective customer, the current resident, and even vendors perceive it.

At the highest levels of your organization these two tasks will get you rolling toward a brand.

1) Decide that the creation of brand strategy should become part of the five-year strategic plan of the organization.
2) Include in the yearly marketing plan what branding goals will be identified and accomplished during that year.

Either you love your current organization's name and want to create a brand that differentiates it from the competitors or you want to start at ground zero and recreate yourself with a new name and brand. The best approach is to hire a branding specialist or have an expert within your organization who has extensive branding experience walk you through this branding process. Do not wing it!

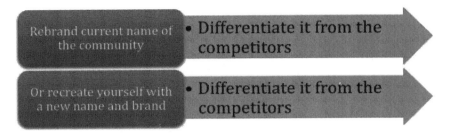

Branding does not happen by magic or osmosis. It is a long, detail-driven process that requires buy-in from all stakeholders within the organization. Maybe you have accomplished some of the hard work already and can skip "Stage 1 Building the Branding" and move directly to "Stage 2 – The Culturalization of Your Brand."

"Stage 1 Building the Branding" in a nutshell:

1) Schedule a branding retreat, led by a branding expert. Make sure your corporate management and key marketing staff attend. (It is very helpful to have the management team read the same branding book prior to the retreat for proper preparation.) The branding expert will need extensive background information to incorporate into this retreat, including:
   a. Determine your organization's SWOT (Strengths, Weaknesses, Opportunities, and Threats).
   b. Identify the strengths and weaknesses of your top three competitors and compare with your SWOT.
      i. How technologically advanced is your company in comparison with the competition?
      ii. What about the age of the physical plant of your community? Have you reinvested enough to give your community a fresh, updated look? Compare yourself to the competition through the eyes of the customer.

iii. Consider the quality and square footage of the apartment homes that the customer can choose from. (Does anyone have granite countertops as a standard?) Do you have too many studios?

iv. Ultimately the customer is selecting lifestyle. How do programming and offerings compare? Does anyone have a complimentary town car service or valets?

v. Wellness is very important to the younger senior. Do you have a pool, fitness instructor, plus a range of classes like yoga, tai chi, and Pilates? Does the competition have them?

vi. Is your dining experience better than average? Does the customer want to come to your community and have a complimentary marketing luncheon to consider the community? If not, why not?

vii. Are you and the stakeholders proud of your community? Would they *truly* like to live there? Do you want your parents to live there? If not, why not?

viii. What is the reputation of your health services? Does everyone in your city have deficiency free surveys? How do you stack up? Does the health center have two-bed rooms or private suites?

ix. Who has the best health services package according to the customer? Are you Type A – life care (pay entrance fee and have the same monthly cost no matter what level of care you need), Type B – entrance fee with discounted health care, or Type C – month-to-month rental?

    x. Which retirement community does the customer perceive as providing the most security protection of future health costs and peace of mind?

   xi. How does your pricing compare? Are you the most or the least expensive? If you have entrance fees, how close are they to the current home values in your city?

  xii. Is your sales staff pushy or educational? Do your customers buy or do they feel they are sold? (People who are sold can have cognitive dissonance later and regret their decision.) Hopefully your competitors appear as used car salespeople.

 xiii. How many rings on average does it take for a live marketing person to answer the phone? How does this measure with the competition?

 xiv. Which retirement community in your area is known for the friendliest residents and staff? Is it yours? If not, why not?

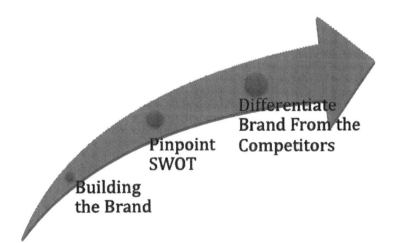

Differentiate Brand From the Competitors

Pinpoint SWOT

Building the Brand

The answers to all these questions further pinpoint your SWOT. If you are weak in any of these areas, then start an initiative with the operational team to correct them before the branding rollout coming in six months or so. Keep asking yourself: How are you different from the competition? How can your organization be perceived as a better choice by each stakeholder?

2) Share the results of the branding retreat at the next quarterly board of directors meeting and make sure to get their buy-in.

3) Take the branding retreat results to a deeper level by having a day retreat with the entire marketing staff and the branding expert. It's vital that salespeople who have direct relationships with the customers are on board with the concept of the brand and believe that the brand ideas actually differentiate you from the competition.

4) Create a branding document that summarizes the branding retreat. Include the ideas of corporate management, the board of directors, and the input from the marketing staff who know the customers better than anyone. Include future focus group questions for residents, vendors, and prospects.

5) Conduct focus groups using a professional focus group moderator with the residents that target the ideas and implementation of the new brand concepts. Determine if they *truly* believe and can relate to the brand. If it is determined that they do not believe, then you must go back and repeat some earlier steps. If they do relate— enthusiastically—then move on to the next step. It's vital

to have buy-in from the residents because 50 percent or more of your new referral leads come from current residents. Please do not discount how important they are to your branding process.

6) Host a luncheon for key vendors and have the branding expert roll out a high-level explanation of your new brand and get their buy-in. They have parents who could someday live at your community. How do they perceive your organization *now* and what do they think of your new brand concept? Watch body language and facial expressions. This is another reason to have a professional brand expert moderate. Does your brand *really* differentiate your organization in their eyes?

7) Ask your marketing staff to suggest a couple of families "moving in" from three groups: Depositors planning to move in within the next several months, waiting list prospects considering your community in the short term

(next six months), and those who say they will someday move to your community (five years). Tell them to choose prospects open to having a complimentary lunch and helping the company with some branding research. You want to be careful to not jeopardize any possible sales. If you do this properly, you can make it fun for the volunteers.

8) The branding expert will compile all this information and create a presentation that summarizes all the findings articulating your brand to make it distinctive from the competition. Think of how useful this could be!

9) A logo, tagline, and general look should be developed through a marketing professional that speaks to your new brand. This same expert can help you with buying media, producing events, developing an ongoing public relations plan, and more. It is not necessary to retain the services of an expensive marketing firm with high overhead.

Now your organization has an appropriate brand name, logo, and tag line, and now you are ready to start the culturalization of the brand within your organization. It's as simple as having everyone within your organization (staff and residents) understand and *believe* your distinct brand. The education process takes time and can be led by your branding expert. This is rolled out simultaneously with new or updated collateral pieces (brochures, website, direct mail pieces, etc.), an advertising campaign, and a grass roots campaign through the residents, management, board of directors, vendors, and staff to their friends, family members, colleagues, volunteers, city officials, and the local chamber of commerce.

"Stage 2 – The Culturalization of Your Brand"

1) Add your new branding image into the presentation created during "Stage 1– Building the Branding." Have your branding expert show it to all the stakeholder groups, including the board of directors, corporate management, executive directors, middle management, marketing directors, salespeople, dining staff, health services staff, maintenance staff, housekeeping staff, concierges, valets, vendors, administrative support staff, and finally the all-important current and prospective residents. This will be the beginning of the branding culturalization process.

2) This presentation also should become part of the human resources employee orientation process.

So now all your current stakeholders have been educated on the brand and every new employee will be indoctrinated upon employment.

3) Great care must be given to update ALL collateral pieces from your organization. This includes all brochures, newsletters, DVDs, direct mail pieces, plus any literature produced by dining services, health services, or the wellness team. Keep checking *every six months* to make sure all the old pieces and logos are no longer in use.

4) External and internal signage needs to reflect the new brand.

5) Community vehicles will need new signage. Having your new brand image driven around town on your bus, van, and any town cars is great exposure. Make sure your bus has your logo, phone number, and website on the back in a black, highly readable font. While someone is waiting for

the traffic light to turn green, they could be calling to learn more about your community.

6) The website needs to speak to your new brand and provide a call to action to either call or e-mail the marketing representatives.

Tip: Business Card Test
Pull out your business card. Put your thumb over the logo. What's left? Basically your name and job title, and probably only your mom or significant other is impressed by that. Your card no longer speaks to the personality (brand) of your company. It could be anyone's company. This test shows how vital your logo is to your brand image. While I am on the subject of business cards, remember to carry your business card with you at all times!

7) Human resources (HR) needs to update every job description and all materials to reflect the new brand. HR needs to be comfortable in enthusiastically touting the brand story to new employees and continue to educate current staff at quarterly employee staff meetings.

8) The marketing staff needs to be coached on to how to tell the story of the new brand and why the organization is so excited to be different from the other communities that the prospect might consider. Please note: Never say anything bad about the competition! Instead, elaborate on your wonderful community.

9) Develop an advertising campaign that is strategically rolled out with a call to action to come to the community and see how it is unique. By the way, there is no such thing as *very unique*. Unique means one of a kind. I have seen multiple communities tout themselves as unique. Stop and think: your community may have a woodshop or a pool. Is a woodshop or pool unique? No. Now, if you have a water slide in your pool with a swim-up bar—that's unique.

10) The creation of a new brand is a public relations opportunity for some free advertising, especially within smaller cities. Create an event that the media will attend so your new brand can be on the morning and evening news. See Chapter 6, Great Events Can Fill Your Building.

Wait! You are not finished yet. Check in with the stakeholder groups *every six months* to re-educate them on the brand. Make sure they have not fallen back into the old brand that was familiar and comfortable while still embracing the new brand.

- Check to make sure all old collateral pieces have been destroyed or archived and are not currently being used at any level within the organization.
- Check in to see what you have accomplished as an organization with yearly (or more often) resident satisfaction surveys that should include learning how the residents are identifying with your brand strategy. Here are a couple sample questions to ask: If your brand is royal treatment of the residents, ask if they feel like royalty. If your brand focuses on active aging, are they pleased with the types and frequency of your activities?

- Hire the type of employees who are customer driven and mentor them and current employees to exceed customer expectations that differentiate you from your competition. Live your new brand strategy every moment of the workday.
- Encourage employees to share verbal customer testimonials with management and corporate staff from guests who are visiting loved ones in residential living, assisted living, memory care, or the health center.
- Create a comment card for guests and residents designed to answer how your brand image is being perceived. Include an easily accessible comment card box. Make sure this card is postage paid and addressed so they can just drop it in the mail if they choose. Train employees to invite guests to fill out the comment cards. These comments need to reach all the way to corporate management.
- Incorporate some of these branding testimonials on the website and keep it updated monthly with fresh ones.
- Continue to evaluate collateral materials and how they speak to your new brand image.

Develop a public relations campaign that showcases your new branding strategy. See Chapter 12 on Media Buying, Public Relations, and Community Relations With a Skinny Piggy Bank.

Every employee, whether salesperson, manager, or spokesperson, needs to tell the story of your unique corporate brand with every single encounter, whether it's one-on-one or at an event with several hundred people. Does each of them have an effective spontaneous thirty-second commercial that differentiates you from your competition? Role-play and test them occasionally.

Chapter 4
Do You Have Proactive or Reactive Marketing?

One of the reasons your occupancy may be down is because you may have reactive marketing. What does this mean? Do any of the following scenarios happen at your community?

- You walk into Bored Brad's marketing office and he's sorting paper clips. He just wants to give a tour but no one is coming in or calling the community.
- When you stop by Blabby Barbara's office, she is on the phone, but you quickly determine that she's talking to a friend and not a potential resident.
- Residents complain to management that phone calls to the marketing department are not returned in a timely fashion to friends they have referred and who are prospective residents. You march right over to Moody Marbella on your marketing team to address the residents' concerns. She responds by changing the subject and, worse, blaming *you* with her explanation, "Events won't work. Low occupancy is not my fault." Do you think she missed the point?

Does this really happen? Yes! Reactive marketing people truly exist and I have worked with some of them. It can be a challenge to determine if the new team you are managing is reactive, but once you know the symptoms it's easy to identify:

Symptom 1) Reactive marketing does not have programs or policies in place to make a certain number of outbound phone calls per day. This means every day.

Symptom 2) After conducting a tour, reactive marketing people *wait* for prospects to call *them* back to say they are interested in moving in. This is really the function of an order taker and not the attitude of a professional salesperson.

Symptom 3) Reactive marketers urge spending money on advertising because they claim they don't have any leads and therefore no new sales.

Symptom 4) Reactive marketers exhibit a lack of urgency to answer the phone within two rings.

Symptom 5) Reactive marketers have a lackadaisical attitude returning phone, web, and social media inquiries.

These reactive marketing teams are waiting for walk-ins and call-ins. They believe the customer should just say, "Yep, here's my deposit. Let's call the moving company right now."

Spending money on new leads is a waste of the marketing budget for a reactive marketing team. If the prospect is slow (which is normal) to make a decision or does not initiate calls with the reactive marketer, that prospect will never be contacted again by a reactive marketing team member. This means that 20 percent to 30 percent of sales can just slip through the fingers of this type of marketer. This really does happen, and it can be affecting your financial performance.

Tip: Hire a professional mystery shopper to analyze whether your marketing team is proactive or reactive. A thorough report can describe strengths and weaknesses of your team.

Here is a real scenario that represents what can happen in a community with a reactive marketing team: A couple began to research three possible retirement communities. They took a tour of each one. When one of the three communities followed up four months later, they discovered that the couple was moving to their competitor. They asked the prospect, "Why?" The response from this lost opportunity? "The community we selected was in constant contact with us, had our best interests at heart, and cared about us as real people."

Do You Have Proactive or Reactive Marketing?

To those of you who do proper follow up, way to go! Just keep doing that and encouraging your team. Patience pays off. It's tough to lose any sale to a competitor, especially when you invested hours, energy, and money. Your database will have the proof of how many "touches" you had with your prospects, either in person, on the telephone, through the mail, or inviting them to events at your community. When you put your heart and soul into a sale and it's lost to a competitor, it can be emotionally devastating. If you can honestly say that you made every possible effort to keep the sale at your community, smile and pat your own back with professional pride. I would be honored to work with you.

Determine if your marketing staff acts as tour guides (reactive order takers) or sales professionals (proactive) who build a relationship, creating urgency for one apartment resulting in a move-in.

A professional sales department is:

- Proactive with the prospects
- Listening and engaging prospects to *learn* their lifestyle needs
- Building value to move into your community
- Continuously following up through phone, mail, events, and tours (Note that I did not say e-mail)
- Persevering until the result is a move-in

A marketing team is really a sales force designed to increase occupancy. This is the bottom line. With proper management and mentoring, any team can be turned into a proactive team. It's vitally important to determine if reactive marketing is the cause of your low occupancy.

Companies have marketing directors to manage a team. Someone ultimately needs to be responsible if the team is not performing, and the marketing director is that someone.

The Salesperson's Responsibilities

A database such as REPS needs to be managed and monitored. When every call result is entered by each salesperson, a lead history can be built. How is each salesperson doing on a *daily* basis? They should be providing their manager with their personal activity report at the end of *each* day. The individual's daily report should show how many:

- Deposits received
- New tours conducted
- New tours scheduled
- Inbound calls
- Outbound calls (Leaving messages does not have the same value as voice to voice contact. I have found that reactive salespeople hide behind, "I left a voicemail.")
- Letters sent
- Personal notes sent
- E-mails sent (Note: only if the prospects actually prefer e-mail)

Important note: Introverted salespeople will claim that an e-mail is equal to an outbound phone call. I disagree with this 100 percent. Nothing can replace building a relationship with talking voice to voice vs. e-mails ping-ponging back and forth. E-mails have their place, but I encourage marketing professionals to respond with a phone call rather than hiding behind e-mails.

Marketing Director Management Responsibilities

Marketing directors wear many hats, but let's just focus here on managing sales activities and the database. The marketing director needs to give the team clear goals on a daily and weekly basis. The team then needs to be monitored to determine if the objectives were reached, and if not, why not?

Celebrate the successes and discuss missed opportunities and attempts. Ask the team for suggestions on how *you* can be helpful. The buck stops with the marketing director, and it shows if you're on the team as a captain who cares. If someone is consistently not producing or refuses to be proactive with his or her "marketing," he or she may need to be replaced. Obviously no stone should be left unturned in trying to mentor this type of salesperson. Most of the time, he or she just needs an example of someone else's success and a cheerleader.

Tip: A very effective strategy that I have used is holding a "best practices conference call" with several marketing teams. If the teams have any competitive spirit, they want to outshine their colleagues. They hear the success of one team's persistent call-outs resulting in increased sales. The low performance team determines quite quickly (without my criticizing them) that more call-outs will result in more sales. This really works like a charm...try it.

The director should generate individual and team reports. Here is a formula: A minimum of twenty outbound calls per day should produce at least ten new tours a week. How many tours does it take for your team to produce wait list deposits? How many of those turn into move-ins? Are the calls outbound or is the salesperson just returning customer calls? Returning calls is important, but outbound calls will make the difference in increasing occupancy numbers. Watch these numbers closely. Outbound calls should include returning phone inquiries and following up from tours to generate new interest now.

 **Tip: Senior health needs can change from month to month with a new physical challenge. If you aren't calling them, your competitor is.**

Executive Director or Administrator Responsibilities

Executive directors need to manage the marketing director to make sure the entire team, including the marketing director, is not in this reactive stage. Make it your business to know how many outbound phone calls and tours are completed on a weekly basis. What are your company's goals? Does everyone on the team know them? Are marketing policies for performance minimums in place? When minimums are exceeded, do you compliment the marketing team and tell them how proud you are? If they are not meeting the minimums *consistently*, what is your plan? You may need a marketing expert to turn the team around.

Typical Inquiry/Response Goals

- Web Inquiries – *One* person should have ultimate responsibility for all web inquiries.
  - o Response within twenty-four hours is mandatory.
  - o On the ball marketing teams call the prospect *immediately*. The person is available now, because he or she just e-mailed the inquiry to you.

 **Tip: You would be surprised how many web inquiries welcome the personal phone call. First, it begins building an immediate personal relationship voice to voice. Secondly, the call usually results in scheduling a tour.**

  - o Technical support can have an automatic e-mail response generated immediately. This response can be creative and include:
    - Thank you for your interest in X Community.
    - We have received your inquiry and want to sincerely thank you for taking the time to visit our website.
    - We promise to answer all of your questions in a timely fashion, and we will be contacting you by phone or e-mail very soon. (Note: "very soon" means within twenty-four hours maximum.)
    - Having a video testimonial that visitors to your website can view is an added touch. (This can set you apart from your competition, or if your competitor is already doing it, why aren't you?)

- o If they say they "just want a brochure," make sure you still call them. Why? You want to begin building a relationship. Calling also ensures that this is truly a qualified lead. Be mindful that some brochure packets cost $10 or more to send. Remember you are working for the bottom line. Be prudent with expensive collateral materials. Giving a brochure to a qualified lead has tremendous value. Sending out a brochure to someone who has no intention of moving to your community is a waste. (They may be looking for a rental community and you only offer the entrance fee model.)
- Telephone Inquiries –
  - o Always respond the same day! (Don't allow Dodging Donald to run out the door because it's 4:45 p.m.)
  - o Is a living, breathing person answering the telephone?
    - Pick up the phone within four rings, preferably two.
    - The marketer answering should have a clear voice that is warm, friendly, and full of energy.

Tip: A mirror on the desk helps them remember to smile, and that smile will come through on the telephone.

- A receptionist can take a message for the marketing team (Important note: Never call the marketing team a sales team to the customer. It will scare them off).
  - The receptionist's goal is to get the prospective guest's name, telephone number, and e-mail address.
  - Here is the language: "Our counselors (note the word choice) are currently helping someone right

now. May I have your name and telephone number? I will be happy to have someone call you just as soon as they are available. What is the best time for you?"

- Or "Everyone on the marketing team is giving a tour at the moment. Let me make a note to have someone talk to you as soon as possible...May I have your name? What is your area code and number? When is the best time to reach you?" (There's a reason the receptionist should not promise that you'll absolutely call the person that day. What if you are in back-to-back meetings until 6 p.m.?)

o What if a recorder is answering the telephone?
Is this really necessary? Live is always better.

- Have it pick up within two to four rings.
- Create a short but informative message that includes warmth, energy, and lets them know their call is important to you.

Effective Follow-Up Inquiry Goals

- Respond to web leads within twenty-four hours.
- Return phone calls the same day. (If it's 5 p.m., return the call and set a phone appointment for the next morning.)

Building Value on the Telephone

Picture this exchange: "How much is a two-bedroom?" The first thing everyone wants to know is the cost, and they often make an immediate judgment of yes they can or no they can't afford it. If you immediately state the price, how can they make a real decision? **The reality is that it is unfair to potential residents to give the price without building value.** They need to know how your community will benefit their future lifestyle and give them peace of mind from health's uncertainties. How much is that worth to them? We are talking about people's lives and futures!

Note: Think of it this way…What if someone were to ask you how much beef costs? Do they mean a cheap, high-fat hamburger to stretch a meal or a lean, tender rib eye steak with just the right marbling for added flavor and tenderness? They are two completely different types of beef for different dining desires…just as no two retirement communities are the same.

First things should be first. If it's your first time talking to the prospective resident on the phone or in person, be sure to get his or her name. Remember you're talking to a human being with a name and personality, and you need to show care and genuine compassion. Ask if the prospect has looked at any other retirement communities or continuing care retirement communities (CCRCs). This is a base line to determine if yours is the first community that has been explored. If the prospective resident has looked at other communities, ask how he or she heard about the competitive community—perhaps a friend or relative lives there. If so, immediately ask how the friend likes it. Maybe the answer is that he doesn't like the food. Now you have ammunition to use in a later close. If the prospective resident has not looked at any other communities, ask how he or she heard about you. This lets you know what marketing programs are working.

If you are the first community the prospective resident is exploring, you must start with an attitude of helpfulness and education. The prospective resident needs to know that all retirement communities are not equal and each one is different. What are his or her needs? What prompted him or her to call *today*? (He/she may have just gotten a new, negative health diagnosis or today is the only day he or she is free because of a golf or bridge schedule.) Get as much information as you can by telephone, but don't interrogate the prospective resident. Keep it conversational. Remember this person called you for a reason. The more you ask questions *and listen*, the more sales ammunition you have. Blabby Betty usually starts touting the food too soon and that may not be the caller's hot button.

Now you want to articulate the strengths and benefits of your community. If you are on the phone, practice ahead of time, to make sure every word is descriptive, flowing, and not boring. Your voice should carry energy, compassion, and a willingness to be of service. If the prospective resident has already been looking, then you'll want to embrace that resourcefulness in researching the options. Mention that the average person looks at three to five communities. This also subtly shows that you know your community is superior. Share what makes your community different and why your brand is unique (refer to the branding chapter in this book – Dare to Differentiate Yourself from Your Competition).

Look at the Goal Chart and identify the goal in your given situation. The highest level to take someone is when a prospect becomes a resident. Except for direct admits to assisted or skilled care nursing, a quick move-in is rare. For someone who is independent and active, it's a long-term process to move in, and it can take anywhere from two months to ten years.

Have a goal set for every activity you do. Create a plan and have goals for *each* prospect. Put the goals in your database so the next time you call your prospects a plan has already been established to take them to the next level. Prospects can fast forward and skip steps, but most people percolate. It is not uncommon to talk to someone by telephone for one year before that person decides to experience a tour. Remember, we are working with different types of personalities, and each reacts in a different way.

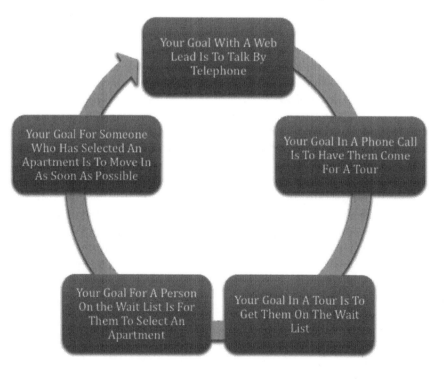

Do You Have Proactive or Reactive Marketing?

The Typical Behavior of the Average Prospective Resident

1. The prospective resident calls or e-mails your community.
2. You speak with him or her (building value) and send out a brochure, if you can't schedule a tour immediately.
3. The prospect calls back to ask for pricing or,
4. You follow up within three days after the prospect receives the packet with new information and continue building value for your community.
5. Invite the prospect for a tour to see (be specific) something you identified in your conversations *that may appeal to him or her*.
   a. If the prospect has concerns or curiosity about the food, invite him or her for lunch or dinner.
   b. If the prospect is the work-out type, invite him or her to use your health club and pool.
   c. If the prospect has voiced curiosity regarding floor plans, invite him or her to come see a few apartments.

Give a "Value Building Tour" (see Chapter 5 - Building Value for Your Community – Giving a Wow Experience!).

6. The prospect will either give you a deposit the day of the tour or send a wait list deposit later (which is more common).
7. Create urgency for immediate move-ins. Talk about the apartment that caters most to the prospect's needs and how it will be your next apartment to be spoken for because of the view, the size, or some other positive attribute.
8. The prospect will indicate if: Yes, he/she can move in immediately or in the next six months, provided he/she sells his/her home or...
9. The prospect wants to wait three-plus years to move in (then continue to engage him/her every six months).

65

10. If the prospect is ready to move in, have him/her select an apartment. (This may take another appointment. Do not drop a prospect like a hot potato because he or she says the move is six months away. Maybe he/she just needs you to connect to his or her emotional needs a little more, so give him/her time to process the move-in. My teams have turned hundreds of these types of people into sales.)

Tip: Watch for signs that your prospect is getting tired. Sometimes you can offer a snack or cup of coffee to revive his or her energy and attention. When scheduling a home selection meeting (or a two- or three-hour appointment), it's best to include lunch after viewing the apartment choices. Then the prospect can perk back up, and all the paperwork can be signed in the same day. It really works like a charm.

11. Encourage the prospect to list his or her home immediately (have real estate resources to help with this).
12. Talk to the prospect every two to three weeks about something new and encouraging. Be the cheerleader until the home is sold (do not pester the prospect, but let him/her know you are there for support).
13. The result? The prospect moves in and says, "Why didn't I do this sooner?" Then be sure to ask for referrals. These types of new residents can be your best allies.

Tip: The value you have built to move into the community has to be greater than the loss of value of your prospects' home when they sell it. They move to have peace of mind with future health concerns and to enhance their lifestyle by taking the elevator to exercise classes, enjoying performances at night again, and eating dinner with new neighbors. They want to stop paying someone to mow the lawn, clean the gutters, wash the windows, and to haul their garbage/recycle containers to the street. The prospects want to have fun in their lives again instead of their home being a ball and chain of responsibility.

marketing2seniors.net

Follow Up – When and How Much?

At the end of the day the difference between a proactive sales team and a reactive sales team is the amount of follow up. Read this carefully to determine where your team lies.

This is by far the hardest part of the sales professional's job. The best part is obviously tours, connecting with the people and having personal sales. The challenge is to have qualified prospects come into your building and then decide to move in. This requires a prompting phone call from you.

After sending a brochure, call the person three days later. If mailing across the country, then call one week later. Look at the information already in the database and work on more discovery with the prospect. The goal is to have him or her come to the community for a tour.

In all fairness, this is what a top marketing professional can experience making calls:

- Recorder machines
- Rude, irritated, or angry people
- Hang-ups
- Feelings of rejection

It can be tough, and the no's have to bounce off you like a beach ball. It's all a game of numbers. If enough calls are made, several people will schedule tours of your community.

The marketing team needs to stay motivated and keep the vision of the company's goals foremost in their minds (100 percent occupancy). Here are some ideas that have really helped my teams:

- Make a hash mark for every call that is made (actually having a conversation with a prospective resident). Before you hit twenty marks, two tours will be scheduled. (This really works! Try it!)

- Start a competition: Whoever schedules the most tours from call-outs (not call-ins) by 3 p.m. gets a reward. (Minimum two tours.) Suggestions: a latte or a smoothie that day (an instant reward that they can enjoy immediately). Having a prize basket that caters to your staff's personal tastes is a caring touch. It might contain a sleeve of golf balls, a $5 gift card to a place they frequent, or a certificate to leave work fifteen to thirty minutes early. Staff loves to be pampered. They will work harder for your praise and surprises than when they are being criticized and put down. Just like listening to your external customer, it's vital to know the hot buttons and interests of your internal customers.

Typical Proactive Out-bound Phone Call Guidelines

Call your prospects:

- Three days after a brochure is sent locally
- Seven days after a brochure is sent across the country

- Three days after a tour to get them on the wait list
- One day after a tour if they are deciding on an apartment home
- Three days after they select an apartment to let them know that you are readily available and will support them through the move. Sometimes people have buyer's remorse, so it's important to check in so that the sale will not disappear.

Proactive Development

When you are not in an existing community, such as one under construction, out-bound phone calls are even more critical as there are no building tours to give. Typically presentations to new prospects are made several times a month at a local hotel by the team of executive/development experts. Contact information for prospects can be gathered at the hotel by offering a door prize or requiring them to share it in order to attend the event.

Marketing teams in the development stage get paid more incentive money to motivate them to spend days and hours on the phone. Yet if they are managed properly, they can generate two hundred to five hundred wait list deposits in one year. An existing community does not command those types of numbers.

Make sure your marketing team is proactive rather than reactive. It is a key to high occupancy. If you are really serious about this, professional mystery shoppers should periodically go through the entire sales process as a prospective resident.

Chapter 5
Building Value for Your Community – Giving a Wow Experience!

Questions to ponder while studying this chapter…

1. **Are you selling real estate or selling emotion?**
2. **Are you just a tour guide or perhaps an order taker?**
3. **Are you justifying the value of the community long before you give the price?**

It's ALL *about building value* to increase your occupancy. Look at it from your prospects' perspective. They love the current home they've enjoyed for the past thirty to fifty years. It's comfortable. They raised their children there. Their grandchildren visit them there. It's where they have celebrated birthdays, anniversaries, holidays, and BBQs. The idea of moving now is daunting. BUT after a hip replacement, a diagnosis of macular degeneration, or a bout with cancer, they feel vulnerable. They may have lost their spouse or know it's imminent in the future. Now they have arrived begrudged at your door. They may feel they are being pushed into a place that will never "feel like home."

Let's start with the kind of tour that does not give value. "Here is the dining room" (you point to it as you walk by), "there is the meeting room," "that's the exercise room and pool," "there's the library, and our bus is on the fritz getting its air conditioning fixed." "Here's one of our twenty available apartments." "People don't like this particular apartment because it's dark."

"Aghhhh!" as Charlie Brown would say. There is no vibrancy of life, no value, and certainly no urgency.

Who would want to move in after a very black and white tour as described in the paragraph above? Where is the lifestyle? Where is the fun? How will living here benefit the prospect? How will doing so fulfill *their* needs? They may as well stay in their home and have someone do their yard work, gutters, and laundry. It's daunting and exhausting to think of packing decades of belongings.

A real tour begins with listening to your customers first. Proper discovery of their needs will identify their hot buttons and desires. People are very capable of buying. They just need enough information from you without feeling that you are being pushy.

You then take the information they share with you and incorporate it in the tour. Every area of your tour should come to life with a lifestyle story. If a resident is not present in the library at the time of the tour, share how this is an extension of the residents' apartment homes and they can enjoy a good book in the library at 2 a.m. if they want. Describe the library committee, for example, and how residents were sitting in the library reading earlier in the day. Caution: don't make up anything. It all needs to be true.

Bring the auditorium to life by sharing stories about the latest fantastic guest performances, lifelong learning, or continuing education events held there. Elaborate on how the residents select the movies that are shown weekly (only if it's true.) Give at least three examples of recent programming and how full the auditorium was. Make these events come to life so they can see them in their mind's eye and wish that they were already there.

Tip: One of the strongest statements you can make is, "A resident (give the name) told me recently that she loves meeting her friends for an evening performance in the auditorium after dinner. When it's over, they just walk back upstairs instead of having to drive in the dark." The next thing is critical: Don't say anything. Let the customer respond. If he says, "Yeah, I don't drive in the dark," or "I don't like going out in the evening," respond simply with "I understand." You just created an emotional connection with him. If he says nothing after one minute, ask him how he feels about driving at night. Very gently, you want him to see the value of evening activities where he won't have to fight traffic in the dark.

Think about what it would take for you to sell your own home and move into the community. This is a good exercise for your own team, as it will help you and them to practice overcoming objections. Paint a vivid and exciting picture of what it's like to be a resident at the community. Why would you want to live there?

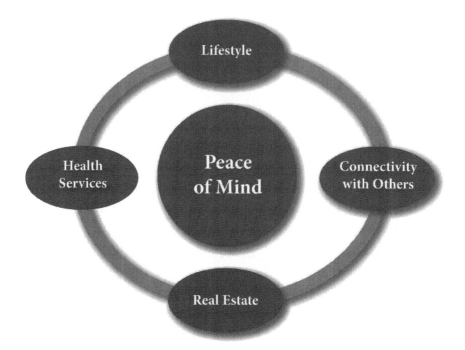

Does your community have more than one treadmill for an exercise program? Hopefully! Build on your community's strengths and share your wellness plan. If you have a pool, make a big deal about it. Is it saline? Saline is so much better for residents' skin and the longevity of their bathing suits. Swimmers know that a swimming suit can easily deteriorate in a chlorine pool, so they appreciate your caring in mentioning it. How many people attend water walking? If no one is swimming in the pool during your tour, then talk about how many residents are lap swimmers or were in classes earlier that day. In other words, if your guest is not seeing vibrant residents, paint the picture of lively group classes.

If the prospect is a swimmer, take the time to describe all the swimming classes you offer unless he or she is just a lap swimmer. Make sure to say that residents love coming downstairs to swim while no longer having to drive in the dark on winter mornings to do so. Wait for a nod or acknowledgement of emotional connecting to this statement before racing on to the next part of the tour. If the prospect doesn't swim, be brief and discuss grandkids swimming during non-class times. I love to say that once grandkids find out you have a pool, you will be very popular. Wait for the smile or nod of acknowledgement before moving too quickly in the tour.

Discover if your prospects are in a current exercise program and what they do now. If your wellness coordinator is available, introduce him or her to your prospect and let them ask this question. Then the wellness coordinator or you can tailor your explanation of wellness programming to the prospects' needs. Maybe they are going to the "Y" now and do some strength training and some cardio on a bike. Show how they can do it in your community but don't have to drive in the snow or rain.

It's great to offer something new in wellness without being pushy. It obviously depends on what programs your community offers. Ask them if they have tried yoga or tai chi before. Share a story of a resident who tried it once he moved in and how he loves it now. Give a real example of how it's helped the resident and how relaxing he finds it. It's not a bad idea for you to attend a few of these classes yourself. Connect with the residents afterward and find out why they keep coming back. Then you can use these quotes in your value building tours.

Interweave "Connectivity with Others" at least twice during the tour!

People have underlying fears of trying a new exercise program. It's easier to continue what they are doing—just as it's easier for them to simply stay in their current home. Ease their trepidations with phrases such as: "The wellness coordinator will walk you through how to use the equipment, and there are new orientation classes for the strength training equipment." Give real examples of how new residents met someone in an exercise class and then made arrangements to connect for a glass of wine in the lounge or had dinner together.

Building Value for Dining

If you just show the dining room and mention the meal times, shame on you! That's Minimal Marvin!

One of a widow's biggest fears is walking to the dining room alone to eat lunch or dinner. Why do you think all the residents line up at 4 p.m. or the earliest your dining room opens? The residents flow into the dining room together and are guaranteed to sit with someone who is starting the meal at the same time. My mom did this every day at the community where she lived. I thought it was bizarre to have dinner at 4:30 p.m., but she said that this was when all her friends ate. Most of her friends were single ladies. My mom never vocalized her fear of eating alone, and her selected eating time was completely unconscious.

Tip: If you want younger and more vibrant residents living in your community, do not schedule tours when all the walkers are lined up outside the dining room. There is no choice, of course, if the prospect just walks in without an appointment. Yet the majority of our prospects do schedule their tour times. Tour prospects when your community looks its best.

Couples have each other to sit with. They have the choice of sitting with another couple, a single person, or dining alone together. A single person may feel like the odd person when eating with a couple or may like it. The point is to present choices. Does your community have a friendship table for singles? If so, share these options when you tour a single. I love to say that when they come to dinner a host or hostess will seat them and no one has ever had to eat alone. Please don't say something such as Insensitive Inez would: "We have a singles' table so all the residents with no friends can eat together." Have compassion for this person who is currently eating every meal alone. Share challenges of healthy cooking for only one or two people. Include examples of real prospective residents who threw out half the head of lettuce when it went bad in his or her refrigerator.

Describe how wonderful your salad bar is and the healthy choices available (we all prefer choices!) Tell the story of how breakfast is easy at home with toasting a piece of bread or pouring milk into a bowl of cereal. Lunch can be as simple as heating some soup, but most people endeavor to eat healthy for dinner with protein, veggies, salad, and some type of starch. "That can create a lot of dirty dishes, right?" Watch for the nod. "When you have dinner here, we do the dishes." If you get that nod acknowledging how much work it is to create a healthy dinner and clean up all the dirty dishes at home, you have made another emotional connection.

Tip: Role-play the use of pronouns in presentations to see what fits your personality. If you tell resident stories and always refer to "them," prospects see "them" as all the old people who live in your community. If they only see walkers and wheelchairs on the tour with you, the prospects won't want to be "them." Some of your stories need to lead into using the pronoun "you." Saying "you" can come off as a pushy salesperson, so don't overuse it. A good place to use "you" would be saying, "Do you like the idea of someone else doing your dinner dishes?" Another service to consider is role-playing consultations. (See www.marketing2seniors.net.)

Some people love to cook, so don't rain on their parade. Instead, be like Wooing Walter and say, "Wow, home cooking is wonderful. Many people here love to cook too, but they told me it's harder to cook for two people instead of a whole family." Pause and wait for them to acknowledge the picture you just painted. Continue, "After their spouses pass away, they decided not to cook every night because they enjoyed eating with their friends in the community here. When their kids and grandkids come over, though, they love to cook for them too." This is fragile territory to cover. You just said, without saying it out loud, "I know you love to cook, but when your husband/wife dies, you will be eating all alone and would have the choice to eat with friends instead of eating by yourself." Be Subtle Sally, not Blatant Betty.

Share how your dining plan has flexibility and choices to fit the prospects' needs. What time do they typically eat now? If your community has assigned seating times, change it to flexible dining hours. It's all about choice and resident preferences, so get with the twenty-first century. The only exception is health care dining because a person needs assistance and therefore needs a planned time.

 **Tip: If you have a famous chef, then tout him or her. Go into detail about all the famous people they have served. My favorite chef cooked for three U.S. presidents, the president of China, and was Bill Gates' personal catering chef for twelve years. He perfected his craft in a Paris cooking school. Start by visiting with your chef and brag about his credentials.**

People love seeing an example of the menu. Is one on display? I'm not talking about a photocopy on a bulletin board. It needs to be displayed in a classy way in an attractive holder or in a leather menu pad. How many evening meal choices are there? There should be at least three. Maybe your community has two entrée choices that vary during the week. In addition, residents could select a hamburger, a piece of grilled chicken, or chef salad if they don't care for the two entrée choices. Well *hello,* that means there are five choices every night. Accentuate your strengths because the competition is trying to show how weak you are.

Tip: Everyone has a fear of getting sick and not having enough food in the refrigerator until they are well enough to go out and resupply. Well, guess what? You have room service, a huge benefit that builds value. It's like insurance. I have fun with room service. Enjoy pointing out, "You get ten complimentary room services per year." Then add, "Someone who is sick could order soup, fruit juice, and tea if they wanted. They can order whatever would make them feel better." Then I laugh and continue, "Most people love using it during the play-off games. They want to stay glued to the TV and not go to dinner that day." Saying something like this makes them realize the community is not just a bunch of old sick people. There are with-it people who like to have fun and purpose in their lives.

Highlight Transportation Benefits

Another fear people have is asking their kids or a neighbor to drive them to the doctor. No doubt you have scheduled transportation to doctor appointments in a certain radius. I talk about these types of benefits as prospects walk down a long hall toward an apartment. This is a trick so that they don't think about how long the hall is.

What types of tours, excursions, or outings does your community offer? Hopefully you have a great program of activities. It builds tremendous value. Always share the top three yearly excursions offered at your community. I like to elaborate on how some people attend the symphony, opera, or ballet whose spouses have always hated going, and now they have a whole new group of friends who all enjoy going to the symphony. Be an extra good listener at this point because they often either agree that their spouse does not like to go or the friend they always went with died or they just can't drive at night anymore. Let them process this. This is another emotional connection.

Does your retirement community offer health services?

There are three types of agreements for the customer to choose from: Type A agreements (Life Care), Type B (Entrance Fee with future health care discounted), and Type C (rent month-to-month). The details on how to strategically market each of these plans depends on your specific competition and your SWOT. I could write another book on this topic alone. The main point is to build value for the strengths of your agreement type.

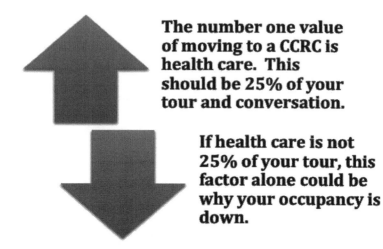

The number one value of moving to a CCRC is health care. This should be 25% of your tour and conversation.

If health care is not 25% of your tour, this factor alone could be why your occupancy is down.

The number one value of moving to assisted living vs. staying at home is health care. If this is not 25 percent of your tour, this factor alone could be why your occupancy is down.

My goal is to build all the value first and then show the prospect an apartment home. It does not always work out that way, but I accomplish it 90 percent of the time. The prospects believe it's all about the real estate (the apartment), but it's not. Real estate is only one component.

My Value Building Tour covers:

1. Lifestyle (how living at the community can make life easier on them so they can enjoy life again—tailor the tour to their interests)
2. Connectivity with others (future friendships, activities with others, and not eating alone)
3. Health services (minimum 25 percent of the tour; it's there when you need it)

4. Real estate (the apartment home or cottage)
5. Peace of mind (now they can sleep better because they have a plan for their future)

How many apartments are available?

Whether you have ten or fifty apartments open, do not tell them. That's what Stupid Stella would do. It won't help you or them. Oh, it's honest, you say??? Well, I say it's not. Read my chapter on Quit Blabbing! Controlling the Flow of Information.

Each apartment is unique. If you have five of the same style apartment available, each one is unique because it's in a different location. It could be on a higher or lower floor, the deck could be different, and the views are definitely different. Each one could have different exposure to the sun.

This is how I do it. They ask, "How many apartments do you have available?" What they are *really* asking is, "Do you have an apartment I would like?" Pay attention here...

This is how I respond: "We have a couple of apartments available in most of the sizes (usually not all sizes are available). The square footages range from 699 to 2,200 square feet. We have one-bedrooms, one-bedrooms with dens, two-bedrooms, two-bedrooms with dens, and three-bedrooms. What size are you interested in?"

Whatever their answer, you say, "Let me make a note of that." Pull out paper and pen to make the note. They just gave you permission to take notes on them. Only write what you want them to see, because they will read what you are writing.

"How much does an apartment cost?"

They may say they want a two-bedroom and follow up with, "How much is it?" If they ask before the tour then they don't qualify for detailed pricing yet, so keep it high level until you have more "discovery" with them. They may have champagne tastes on a beer budget. Say something like, "Pricing is based on square footages and heights in the building (only if it is). One-bedrooms start in the X thousands, two-bedrooms start in the X thousands." Then shut up! What they say next is key.

- They may say, "Oh, I would like to look at one-bedrooms." That tells you they could be very price sensitive. Continue your discovery process, but you may only end up showing them three one-bedrooms today.
- If they ask, "How much are the one-bedrooms with dens?" That may mean they want more space but your two-bedroom price was too expensive for them.
- If they ask, "How much are the two-bedroom with dens and the three-bedrooms?" they are not scared of the two-bedroom price. Find out what their top price is by giving the range of pricing from your least expensive two-bedroom with den to the most expensive apartment in the building. It's really fun to work with someone when money is no object. The challenge can be when one of your prime apartments is not available.

Let *them* push up the price point

Never ever just show someone a two-bedroom because they said they wanted one and then give them the price. Again, that's what Stupid Stella would do. It's like holding out a carrot to a horse and ripping it away. It's mean. They don't want to lose face and say, "Diane, I can't afford this. Will you show me something smaller?" Instead they will leave and go to another community that handles pricing better than you.

First, establish that they are interested in a two-bedroom and give them the starting price point. The next step is to fine tune what they might be interested in and what they can afford, **because you are only going to show them three apartments.** If you show more than that, you will not sell them that day. Period. Trust me, it overwhelms them. Every six to nine months, in a weak moment, I have *allowed* someone to pressure me to show them more than three apartments. When they leave, I always have a talk with myself about showing only three apartments. It's hard when they are demanding, so you must be strong. Know what works. Be better at your discovery, so pick your three best apartments to show them. It's like a bride who wants to try on every dress in the shop. Better to determine if she would even look good in a strapless or princess style.

Use Discovery to Determine Apartment Style Preferences

I ask people if they prefer morning sun or afternoon sun. Every community has four sides to their buildings. Each side has its own strengths, so we are only discussing strengths now. "Would you prefer facing east with morning sun or southern exposure, which has the most light in the winter? West is afternoon sun and north has (give it your strength)." Then shut up and let them process this. Wait for an answer and make a note of it. Ask if they prefer facing toward the street or facing the courtyard, for example. Do they prefer a higher or lower floor?

You must be very careful asking fine tuning questions. For example, if you don't have any apartments facing west, then leave that out. Don't mention your most popular apartments on the ground floor facing the park for pets, if they are all filled. It's mean to dangle something out there they can't have. Practice, practice, practice and role-play different scenarios.

Once you have determined through discovery what their preferences are, decide which three apartments you will show them. Do not tell them which ones. Simply say, "I have three apartments that may suit your needs perfectly. Let's go see them." They will happily follow. Go to the first apartment on your list. See what their reaction is. If it's positive, they are hopefully mentally placing their furniture in the apartment. They may say it's missing this or that needs to be bigger or smaller. Hopefully this is in the layout of the next apartment you are going to show them. While you are in the first apartment you may realize that they have entirely different needs than you originally thought. Adjust the next apartment if necessary to fit their lifestyle.

Your prospects could have a negative reaction as well. Please remember they don't want to leave their 2,000- to 4,000-square-foot home to move into a 1,200-square-foot apartment. It does not mean it's all over. They need to adjust. A proper "value building tour" really helps offset this reaction. They need to realize that the apartment is their own private space for just themselves, but that all the community spaces such as the library, the pool, and the health club are part of their home as well. They can still get away from each other and have some independence. This point needs to be laid down before you show the apartment home. It's too late to bring it up now. Chalk up your mistake and do better on the next tour.

Tip: If you just show them an apartment first, without building value and an emotional connection, you all lose. Who wants to live in a 1,200-square-foot apartment for the rest of their lives? Conversely, who wants peace of mind with health care security? Who wants to simply walk downstairs in the evening for performances? Who wants easy access to dine with friends? Who wants to not drive in the dark on a winter morning to exercise? Who wants the ease of no yard work or climbing ladders anymore? People will overcome the real estate issue to gain all the emotional connectivity.

Don't forget to mention the peace of mind that residents have in case something happens to their health or their spouse's health. You want them to feel there are no grey areas or loose ends. If they move in, they can sleep most peacefully knowing all the decisions have been made. They never have to be a burden to their kids or have someone "put them somewhere." NO ONE ever wants to be "put somewhere."

Finally, ask open-ended questions that motivate them to share their needs and wants with you. Be a good listener and try to incorporate their lifestyle into your tour. Customize each tour based on the discovery of that person or couple. Be engaging and build value at all times. Sometimes it's most valuable if you are quiet and let them process something emotional. They won't move to *just* real estate. They need an emotional connection, so create this on your "value building tour."

Chapter 6
Great Events can
fill Your Building

Are you afraid of events or do you embrace them? How innovative are your events? Are they attracting *qualified* prospects to your community? The sole purpose of events is to have *new* prospects walk in your door and say, "Wow! This is where I want to live." This chapter goes into detail on ideas and how to put on a great event.

What is your definition of an event? For example, the community picnic is a wonderful celebration for all residents and *their families*. It is not an appropriate event to invite prospects because they don't want to see the sea of wheelchairs and walkers from the assisted living and skilled nursing residents. Please do not call this a marketing event. The community picnic is an event for existing residents and should be handled by resident services/activity directors. Marketing directors can help, but they need to stay focused on new sales or there won't be any.

So how many marketing events should you be having? My recommendations:

- Large events should be held three to four times a year.
- Small events should be one to two times a month, depending on occupancy needs and your ability to attract new faces.

Let's break each of them down from start to finish for ideas and planning to produce effective events.

A large event draws one hundred to three hundred attendees. Who do you invite? First on your guest list is your wait list. There are people percolating on your wait list who just need a subtle push to call the moving van and order change of address cards. If your event is done properly, it should result in three to five move-ins in the next quarter. Secondly, one-third of your guests must be new faces. These will come from two sources: advertising and resident referrals. I recommend a quarter page ad in your local newspaper. Please see recommendations for a newspaper ad in Media Buying, Advertising, Public Relations, and Community Building with a Skinny Piggy Bank. The third group to invite is friends of the residents. Many communities get 50 percent or more of their new leads from resident referrals.

Tip: The best way to get resident referrals is to let residents know that they have an opportunity to attend this fabulous event if they bring a guest who is interested in moving to your community. Hello? Knock, knock? Many of your residents' friends probably qualify age-wise and financially to move to your community. Start informing the residents two months ahead of the event.

Tip: Make the event something exciting enough that residents will be able to enthusiastically endorse it and want their friends to attend. Do not have the CEO or a botanist describing the cross section of a leaf to be the main speaker. You may as well have an event to watch your newly painted walls dry. No offense to CEOs, but you are not a big enough draw. A resident's Disney family vacation slide shows are for the residents to see, not your prospects. That theme will make your guest feel grumpy, dopey, and sleepy. Now if you wanted to invite the real Mickey Mouse and give away a trip for two to Disneyland...but that might be too expensive and that would be goofy.

To summarize your event attendance goals:

- Approximately one-third new faces
- One-third wait list members
- One-sixth will be second looks (their second time in your community)
- Less than one-sixth will be residents (who have invited a new face guest)

Planning should start a minimum of three months before the event date. Begin planning with the end result in mind. An event starts with an idea...

General Theme Ideas

- "Antiques Road Show" (guests get one or two items appraised)
- Vibrant gardening expert sharing tips on container gardening
- Fascinating speaker who is a resident's relative, such as an astronaut, an Olympian, or an entertainer
- Mayoral debate
- State pageant winner, such as Miss (Your State)
- Car show (this can be combined with other events to draw men)
- Engaging speaker on health or wellness (get a local expert from a gym or hospital)
- "Resident Home Showcase" (five to eight residents open their homes and you provide "passports" that are stamped for prizes)

Financial and Real Estate Themes

- "How to Sell Real Estate Now"
- Financial planner (include examples of why moving to your community is good)
- "Capital Access Seminar" (how they can move in without selling their home yet)

Music and Cultural Themes

- An opera performance by a local school
- Outdoor summer concert series
- Resident drama group performance (must be great)
- Steel drum band (guests can wear Hawaiian shirts complete with leis donated by your community)
- A local child prodigy who has been accepted at a famous school of the arts

Great Events can fill Your Building

- Jazz group from a local college
- Caribbean island party with themed music, food, and staff costumes
- "Big Band Night" or a "Sock Hop" (bring in local dance instructors to dance with the guests)

Holiday Themes

- Live Nativity (if you are a Christian-based organization)
- "The Dickens Carolers," Father Christmas, or school group singing carols
- Celebrate Veterans Day or Memorial Day
- Thanksgiving luncheon with live music (Monday of Thanksgiving week.) Do you know how many people have family in other parts of the country and are lonely during the holidays?
- Valentine's Day celebration with music and homemade chocolate
- St. Patrick's Day Irish dancers, Irish soda bread, and tea
- Mother's Day – high tea (during the week before the actual day)

Communities in Development Event Ideas

- Lotteries (to determine the order of who selects apartments first)
- "Meet the Architect" and see floor plans unveiled
- Meet the design team so future residents can give input on the building's interior
- Ground breaking ceremony (complete with a tent, sound system, music, and a live band)
- Wine tasting to select wines for the dining room
- Microbrew tasting
- "Meet the Chef"

- Meet your new neighbors (floor by floor events)
- Hard hat tours of the building

Plus you will have grand opening celebrations for brand new or renovated areas. These are VERY popular. People love to see what's new.

Tip: If you don't have the time or the people power to organize a major event, then engage the services and resources of a professional event specialist who understands the senior mindset. Relieve your pressure. I discovered a national organization that can do all the legwork for usually less money than I can do it myself. Let me know if you need some help: www.marketing2seniors.net.

What is the timing of an effective program?

Introduction – three to five minutes

The introduction should include welcoming everyone, something humorous, and introducing the theme.

Theme – twenty-five to thirty minutes

Your theme draws the prospects, and its presentation should last twenty to thirty minutes. I know what you're thinking: I'm paying $500 for this band and they're only playing for twenty-five minutes? No! Tell the musical group that they will play for twenty-five minutes to *start* your program, then have some speakers for about twenty minutes, and when the guests start enjoying the food (themed for your event) they can play again for thirty to forty-five minutes. Having music during the eating portion of the event really creates a fun atmosphere. It rounds out the theme and brings it full circle with the food you've selected.

Resident Testimonial – five-minutes

Select a younger-looking, enthusiastic resident. Tip: Tell him or her to talk for four minutes (because they always go over) and focus the talk on your purpose for the day.

Two to Three Stories – five to ten minutes

The marketing director and/or administrator should share a couple of quick stories about why your community is different and exciting. First—and this is very important—ask for a show of hands of how many people are seeing the community for the first time. Hopefully it's one-third of the room. You will be able to determine how many people are there from the wait list and from your RSVP list.

- Briefly cover the value parts of the community that they would see on tour that they can't see today. This will depend on where in your community you are hosting the event. For example, "Today we are currently in the auditorium, which is used for everything from pickle ball (smile and say "but obviously all the chairs are removed and the net is set up") to last week when we had the U.S. ambassador to Iraq here talking to our residents. It was fabulous (smile)." (Please note: This is an example of an exciting event for "with-it" people.)

"We have great programming here (smile). A resident told me last week that she loves events in the evening because she doesn't have to drive in the dark (smile)." Then mention the saline swimming pool, the health club, the library, and multiple dining venues and then highlight the lounge that had a limerick contest on St. Patrick's Day when almost everyone wore green (for example).

- Perhaps your administrator can cover how the residents had an event to raise money for the foundation. The foundation is designed for residents who out-live their resources. Some people don't anticipate living one hundred years or more and it gives people peace of mind to know the foundation is there just in case. This is something they can share later with their protective children.

- Share how a new renovation is making a difference in the residents' lives.

- Describe a recent resident trip to watch whales, visit a kangaroo farm, or something unusual that average people don't do on their own.

- The health care administrator (*only* if he or she is a good speaker) or administrator can say something positive; for example: "We just had a deficiency-free survey in our skilled nursing care," or "We have just gone to electronic record keeping" (and what this means) or "We are proud to have celebrated the 105th birthday of one of our residents" (who resides in health services). "Maybe you saw her in the newspaper? She claims it's from eating our scrumptious mashed potatoes and drinking coffee every day." (Humor is fantastic if you can swing it with a health care story).

Tip: At each event, make a point to draw out and accentuate two reasons to move. Give specific reasons for people to move from their home and live in your community. One story should always focus on lifestyle (how living here can make their lives easier and more enjoyable). The other can rotate between connectivity with others (perhaps one of them is alone in their home after the spouse passes away), health services, and peace of mind. The point is to not make it sound like you are selling! But you must take the time to remind them of the value reasons to move here. Do this and you will have guaranteed move-ins in the next few months!

What's Coming Up Next and Thank the Musical Group – five minutes

Explain in detail what will be happening next on the event's agenda. Share what the themed refreshments are, where they will get them, and where they can sit to enjoy them.

Tip: You can give theme names to mundane dishes, which makes it more fun. Musical themed food could be something like "Flapper Frittatas" (for a roaring twenties' theme), hot dogs could be "Frank Sinatras" (for a big band night), salmon could be "Salmon Chanted Evening" or chicken drumsticks could be simply "Drumsticks," giving your food a musical theme. Engage your chef and have fun with this.

If appropriate, talk about your chef and introduce him or her. Let him/her elaborate on what has been prepared especially for them— if the chef's personality is extroverted. If not, share what they will be enjoying and encourage the chef to at least make an appearance and wave. Let your guests know tours of selected apartments are available and will start in thirty minutes. You must show three great apartment homes. First impressions are everything. If your empties are not stellar, then have six good-looking, able-bodied residents show their beautiful apartments. (Preview them first to make sure they are not overcrowded or unappealing.)

The entire program will be forty-five to fifty-five minutes, not including the themed refreshments after the program. Hopefully people will stay for the tours, but they don't have to.

Costs for Events

Most themed events can be put on for very little money, in my opinion. Themes can range from free (residents' famous kids, a local school musical group, a child prodigy) to a required donation around $500 (for a college opera or musical group) to $1,000 or more for a professional musical group. "Antiques Road Show" can be the most expensive as it takes several professional appraisers to appraise two hundred or more items.

Your biggest unknown cost is food. Lunch is the most expensive proposition. I don't really recommend lunches for themed events. You want to give them a GREAT bite to eat (small plate) and then offer tours. It takes too much time to eat a whole lunch and then they are too tired and go home. You have about two hours before they start to fade and are mentally fatigued.

Great Events can fill Your Building

Food really varies with each community and how the dining department charges for catering. If they only charge the marketing department for food costs, say, "Yahoo." Paying for the labor and servers obviously has higher costs. My target is $5 to $10 food cost per guest with a lot of negotiating to keep costs down and quality up, especially if the caterers charge you for labor. That means that with one hundred guests, your event can cost $500 to $1,000. It's vital that the food is fantastic and that it represents what the guests will be eating when they move in. (Note: I said *when* and not *if* they move in. Part of your success includes your positive mindset.)

Other Costs

Holding the event in your own community keeps costs controllable. You should not have to pay for renting chairs, tables, linens, plates, cups, glasses, serving utensils, a sound system, a stage, microphone, AV equipment, screen, or parking. These can easily cost around $5,000 to $10,000 in a metropolitan area, with the largest costs being parking and full AV equipment. The most I ever paid for parking was $20 per car in downtown Seattle for a lottery event at a hotel. Now I look for venues that will only charge $5 to $8 maximum for parking to keep costs reasonable.

Are You in Development?

Parking and food are formidable costs for your events. Always pay for parking and always give guests almost a full brunch or lunch. No tour is given (because your building is not yet built); therefore, you want to engage with them as long as possible. Make sure the location you select has easily accessible restrooms. Please consider your guests' total walking distance from their cars to the event in the building to restrooms and back to their cars. It should not be more than two or three blocks each way.

Ground breaking events can cost $15,000 to $25,000 because they are outside and you have to rent everything including portable potties. A tent is vital because you have to be prepared for weather, which may be windy, too hot, or rainy. I never recommend a ground breaking during the winter; it's flat out too difficult and too expensive.

Weather

Nothing stops future residents from attending an event like snow. In one of my first event jobs, we spent $20,000 for a fabulous event and got snowed out. We were supposed to have 1,000 kids attending and we had 150. It was disheartening to put on a pyrotechnics show for so few people. My advice: Do not have high-priced events in the winter. Have the antiques show or higher-cost performers in the fall, spring, or summer.

Step-By-Step Event Planner Guidelines

So let's pick an event and organize the whole procedure with easy-to-follow instructions. Let's select a jazz trio from your local college for a May or June event. Please note: College instructors will usually only permit their students to perform at the end of a quarter, so plan ahead. It may take a year in advance to plant a seed with the school for a performance at a later date. High school instructors usually have their students for the entire year, so they may do something for the holidays or hold a spring concert for you.

Great Events can fill Your Building

One Year in Advance

- Put events in your budget

Four to Five Months before the Event Date

- Brainstorm ideas

Three Months before the Event Date

- Contact the college to find out when the end of their quarter is and when final exams are to determine if your event should be in May or June. Ask the cost. It's usually a donation. Sometimes they ask for $100 per student if it's a jazz trio, for example.
- The instructor tells you a Tuesday in May around 1p.m. will work for his students. You can get back to him with an exact date later.
- Check with resident services (or the activities department) and make sure you have your event location reserved.
- Make sure the administrator, resident speaker, and any other speakers will be available on that day.
- Talk to dining services directly about your theme and get an estimate on your food budget that coincides with your projected budget for this event.
- If any key people are on vacation, pick another Tuesday (for example).
- Call the college instructor and lock in the date.
- Do not schedule around Memorial Day weekend or other holidays. Be sure to check sporting events schedules in your area. They may conflict and affect your attendance, traffic, or parking.

Two Months before the Event Date

- Contact newspapers to start working on an ad and negotiate pricing. Local, well-read newspapers are the best. Do not dismiss small town weeklies as they are often more widely read than large dailies. See if they can provide the demographics of their senior readers.
- Design invitations to include:
  o Guest speaker/performer
  o Theme
  o Where (your address and the location in your building)
  o When (date and time, including the ending time)
  o How to's (where to park, directions, entrance, etc.)
  o RSVP date with a contact phone number is a must or your budget will be broken trying to guess food needs. The RSVP date should be five days out from the event day. Please note: Your date to provide food estimates to the chef is usually three days before. (Trust me you will need the wiggle room.)
  o Graphics should play to your theme.
  o Add an element of fun, but always be classy (spelling, font, color, paper quality, etc. are vital elements).
  o Do not say there will be introductions or that the administrator will speak.
- Determine which invitation formats to use:
  o Flier (8.5 x 11) with #10 envelope
  o A community note card with the message inside and small envelope
  o Oversized postcard (this costs the most, but the prospect could be throwing away your community's envelope

mailings.) Advantages are the ability to use two sides and no envelope.

- Call the college instructor to discuss music, timeline, and getting W-9s for the students (if you are paying individual students vs. a donation to the school). *You are really making sure they have the date locked in before you mail the invitations.*

- Schedule an appointment with your dining director or chef to discuss the menu in detail. Treat them with the respect they deserve and the catering will be better than the nicest hotel in your town. My typical menu has a protein, fruit, salad (pasta), and dessert. It can be all in appetizer form or presented in very small portions. Remember to name everything around your theme.
  o Always use china unless it's an outside event.
  o Always have plenty of coffee, even if it's warm weather.
  o Always have ice water.
  o Don't forget tea enthusiasts.
  o A nice punch, lemonade, or iced tea is lovely in warm weather.
  o Use smaller plates.
  o Consider diabetics and don't serve all sugar. Offer a fruit and a protein.
  o Foods that don't require knives are best.
  o No pork if you have possible Jewish or Muslim guests.
  o Stick with chicken and fish as the protein unless you are in a beef state such as Kansas or Texas.
  o Buffets are usually the easiest, but make sure they are on a "fluffed table."

o   If you can, have two food lines or arrange food on smaller separate tables for improved traffic flow. No one likes to wait in line.

o   Include fresh flowers somewhere.

o   Do not serve the same food as at your last event.

o   Grand openings will need ice sculptures.

- Get invitations to the printer six weeks out (they need to be mailed one month out).

One Month before the Event Date

- Mail invitations (it's vital they are four weeks out).

- Invite selected residents to show their homes. Explain in detail that they will take two groups of ten to fifteen to their homes and that every light needs to be on.

- Meet with staff directors individually and let them know how much you need their help with this event and how it will help to fill the building.

    o   Get volunteer staff to assist with registration and greeting guests. Your business manager or activity director could be a great help.

    o   A volunteer is needed in the parking lot to direct people to the event entrance. Have balloons at the entrance to tie in with your theme. For example: A fiesta theme would use red, green, and white balloons.

    o   Make a scheduled appointment with your head maintenance person (most places call him or her a facility director. I abhor this word because no one wants to live in "a facility"). Discuss the following:

        ▪   Date and time of your event

- Having the set up completed the day before (if possible).
- Table for registration with two chairs and an attractive garbage can
- Tables for the food buffet (FYI—linens will need to go on two hours before the event for the dining staff to fluff and make showy)
- Discreet garbage cans in food area
- Chair set up
- AV set up (A small table may be needed for this and the seating adjusted to accommodate the table)
- Consider heat or air conditioning needs depending on the weather and the number of guests
- Sound checks the morning of the event for the speaker
- Who will adjust the microphone volume at the event?

o Talk with the director of housekeeping or environmental services
- Discuss the traffic flow to all locations your guests will be going (including touring apartments) so their staff can give extra attention to those areas before and during the event.
- What restrooms will be used the most? Housekeeping should check in the middle of the event to make sure they are clean and restocked.

o Talk with your administrator about how important his or her speaking role is at the event and what he or she needs to accentuate.

- Start making signage if needed (from the parking lot or within the building).
- Set the program with the school and discuss the number of songs and time limit. If possible, schedule them to play additional music while the guests are eating.
- Speak at the resident council meeting about this event. Invite residents to attend if they bring a guest who could potentially move into the community (not someone's daughter, for example, unless she is a real prospect).
- Post a flier about the event and how residents can attend (by bringing a guest who will potentially move in). Put one in each resident mailbox, do an e-mail blast, make an announcement on the resident TV station, or however you can communicate with the majority of residents. (It needs to be the talk of the dining room at dinner.)
- Order the newspaper ads. Some publications only publish once a month or once a week and have long lead times. Get in the free upcoming events section too!
- Designate someone to be the photographer for your event. This must be the photographer's sole responsibility. You can use those photos later for newsletters, websites, social media updates, etc. If it's a huge event, such as a grand opening, hire a professional photographer.
- Post events on your website and other social media before and after the event.

Two Weeks before the Event Date

- Make sure you have not forgotten anything—review the checklist.

- If any of your resident volunteers or speakers were on vacation, bring them up to date now.
- Order flowers for the registration table and find out if the dining staff needs some for their display.
- Prepare inquiry guest cards, registration basket, and drawing. (If residents have a new guest attending, you will want to capture their information. It's rude to say, "May I have your information?" Instead have them fill out a card so they can be entered in the drawing for prizes. Give several $20 gift cards for a local restaurant or maybe offer the flower displays on your registration table and/or dining tables that they can take home at the end of the event.)
- When collecting RSVPs, get as much info as possible. Say, "Oh, will there be two of you then? Please allow me to spell your names correctly (including first names) for the nametags." (They need to know this is an official event.) Ask, "What is your phone number?" (Just ask. The worst they can say is no). After I get their names, I say, "Mrs. Jones, your phone number is 206—??" (Or whatever your area code is with a question mark in your voice. They just fill in the rest of the number automatically.) Continue, "And your address is?" That is all you need for now. Thank them and let them know that they can invite a friend or neighbor to come. Ask them to please call you back as soon as possible, to make sure there is enough food for everyone. Conclude with, "It will be a lovely event that I know you will enjoy." Give any parking instructions if needed.
- Put RSVPs on an Excel spreadsheet (or some other program) to count people. You can't just count names. Some people are singles and others are bringing two guests. This is vital to

keep your food costs down and to set up the proper number of chairs.

- Prepare a check request for the musical group or musicians so you can present them with a check on the day of the event. You will find this promptness builds a relationship with them for future events. They may market you to their friends because of your professionalism.

- Give a status update of the RSVP date for your event on Facebook and other social media. Try to freshen the message so it's different from the initial message about the event.

One Week before the Event Date

- Meet with key management staff to walk through the event and talk about overlapping roles. Examples: Maintenance is setting up the buffet tables, and dining services needs it completed by a certain time so they can prepare their display to set out the food. Explain which apartments will be toured and share a brief description of the program and how each of their roles is vital to the success of this marketing event. Let them know how much you appreciate each of them and their staffs. Be sincere, smile, and say thank you! Let them know how many people have RSVP'd so far and be enthusiastic.

- The majority of your RSVPs should be in now. Do you have enough? Does your marketing team need to make calls to invite hot prospects or wait list members who have not RSVP'd? I have had fifty to one hundred more people attend an event with this successful method. I know you are busy, but you want as many qualified prospects as possible to attend. Attendance is your main task before an event, so take the time to get as many attendees as possible. It will increase your occupancy.

- Start preparing nametags. Alphabetize them by last names.
- Check in daily with the dining department or chef with total number of attendees.
- Call the school instructor to find out what time the musicians are arriving and advise where they can park.
- Start writing your remarks for the program.
- Give a status update of door prizes and compose a last chance to RSVP for your event for Facebook and other social media.

Three Days before the Event

- Give dining the final food count (do not pad with additional people). A few more people may RSVP, but you will have just as many no shows or cancellations. Dining normally makes 5 percent extra food. If your count is 150 and 160 show up, there will be enough food and they can charge you for 160 people. If you say 160 and 145 show up, then you still have to pay for 160. Protect your budget. Please note: The dining department will either respect your estimate of people after the first event—or not. Get a reputation for being accurate.
- Nametags and registration should almost be done now.
- Finish your speech and start rehearsing. Practice in front of a mirror, a trusted friend, or videotape yourself.
- Confirm with the photographers and let them know what types of pictures you would like to capture. You may want to show them examples, both good and bad.

Two Days before the Event

- Send a flier or letter to all the residents who have agreed to show their apartments. Thank them and remind them to please turn on every inside light (including the bathrooms and closets) before they come to the program. The apartments need to be lit before the guests walk inside.
- Call maintenance and give them the final numbers for chairs in the auditorium.
- Go over your checklist again. Have you forgotten anything?

The Day before the Event

- Are you buying the flowers yourself? If so, get them today and run any other final errands.
- Nametags and registration should be printed and organized alphabetically.
- Lay out everything for the registration table.
- Call your resident speaker to see if he or she needs a pep talk.
- Tell your administrator how confident you feel that everything is ready and thank him or her for the support.
- Get a good night's sleep.

 **Tip: There can be many pitfalls to creating a fantastic event, but proper preparation takes care of 99.9 percent of them.**

The Day of the Event

- Is the room laid out properly?
- Count the chairs.
- Is the microphone ready to go? Have a sound check for *yourself*.
- Set up the registration table with linens and flowers. Does it have two chairs and an attractive, discreet garbage can?
- Registration should have inquiry cards for unregistered guests. Guests pre-registered and in your database only have to put their name at the top of the inquiry card to be in the drawing. Unregistered guests need to fill them out completely. Ask how they found out about your community. Try to determine if they are interested in moving in soon, in six months, one year, or two years plus.
- Have the flowers arrived?
- How is dining doing with their set up?
- Check the restrooms to make sure they are perfect. Is there extra toilet paper? Check the soap and towel supply. Is the trashcan pristine? How does the room smell? Is there a freshener?
- Have your speech with you.
- Have your cell phone with you.
- Forward your office phone calls to the receptionist so you can get cancellations *noted in writing* by a live person. Tell the receptionist that you don't want to know about attendees until after the event. They are only to call you if, for example, the school instructor, the musicians, or the florist can't find the community.

- Do not answer your phone once the event begins. Turn it off. It's rude to leave it on! Be there 100 percent for your guests.
- Lay out the nametags for guests to pick up and put on.
- Last minute attendees will get their nametags through your registration helpers after they fill out an inquiry card (tell the guests it's their ticket to enter the door prize drawing). If they balk, add that nametags are for security purposes, since they are guests in your community. NO one says no to that!
- Be *completely* ready one hour before the event.
- Have your registration people ready one hour before.
- The parking attendant (volunteer) needs to be positioned forty-five minutes to one hour before the event starts.
- Greet your musicians and help them with any additional needs or microphone checks (I insist that they do microphone checks forty-five minutes to one hour before the event. It is rude to do microphone checks right before the program starts. It makes *you* look unprepared.)
- Show the photographer where to stand and what angles you want to capture. Ask for photos that show the energy of many people in the room. Avoid shots that have several empty chairs in them.
- Have check or checks ready to hand to the musicians or the group leader.
- Wash your hands, check your clothing, brush your teeth and reapply your lipstick (ladies only?).

When Guests Arrive

- Smile and greet people.
- The administrator should be smiling and greeting people too.

- Make sure you are free to talk to people. You may have five people tell you before the event that they want to talk to you about moving in soon. Memorize these names! Discreetly write them down at your next opportunity.

During The Event

- Enjoy your intro and remember to smile!
- While the musicians are playing, write down any important notes from greeting people.
- Hopefully dining has made an outstanding display that is completed. Note: If your buffet is in the same room, it is rude to have dining setting up during the program.
- COUNT how many people are attending. Trying to guess after the event is unprofessional.
- Take a few moments to enjoy the program and decide what complimentary comment you will use to describe the musicians when you thank them from the microphone.
- Glance at your prepared remarks.
- Don't allow registration people to be distracting when interacting with latecomers (the program is on so they should whisper).
- Introduce the resident speaker. Keep it short, but say something interesting about him or her. This is another element to making your event more memorable. After guests go home, they may not remember exactly what you said but will reflect on having had a good time.
- Introduce the administrator, who may or may not be speaking. (If speaking, make sure he or she says something to edify you.)
- Give closing remarks on what will happen next.

- Hold the door prize drawing. Make it fun! Don't be like Dan the Dud and just do a deadpan drawing.

After The Program

- Make sure you work the room and talk to every single person at this time. Maybe you can talk to them while they are in the buffet line. Ask them how they are and be genuine.
- Thirty minutes later call out tour groups for different-sized apartments (not everyone wants to see a one-bedroom and others don't want to see big ones they can't afford).
- Write notes discreetly.
- Never leave the room. Everyone should know where to find you at all times.
- Keep smiling until the last guest has left.
- It's time to clean up.
- Take all leads and notes to your office *immediately* for the follow up tomorrow.
- Critique the event while it's fresh in your mind. Write a few notes on what worked and what didn't work. Did you get enough new people?

The Day after The Event

- Send out a thank you e-mail to all staff volunteers and let them know how their participation made a difference to the success of the event. The administrator loves to respond to this type of e-mail and put in his or her two cents. Department heads can be proud of their front line staff and share your e-mail with them. State some specific examples such as, "Everyone was raving about the pasta salad," or "The restrooms were spotless for the entire event."

- Send out a personally hand-written thank you to each resident who either spoke or showed their apartment. If your budget allows, give a small gift, such as a tin of cookies or a certificate for a free dinner guest.
- Call back anyone who asked a question at the event and who you promised you would contact.
- Check your inquiry cards. How did people find out about the event? Did they see your website, social media, newspaper, hear it from a friend, or was it a resident referral?
- Take notes to make improvements for next time.

Two Days after The Event

- Call new prospects, thank them for coming, and find out when (not if) they would like a personal tour to look at apartments. They will immediately tell you their time frame. Make a note of it in your database and try to get as much information as possible, such as how they found out about the event and do they have any friends who live in the community.
- Go through photos for "keepers." Save them for the next newsletter or to post on your website or social media (don't forget to get written permission to use someone's photo). You may even want to send them out to a prospect.

Five Days after The Event

- Call new prospects again who were not home the first time you attempted to reach them. Make sure you leave encouraging and uplifting voice messages. If they are not home, schedule the next call in two weeks.

- Did you thank *everyone*?

Every event is a learning experience for the next one. Here are a few event bloopers that even the best of us have experienced at one time or another:

- Forgetting to give an RSVP date in the invitation. It was tough to guess how much food, so I had overages in food and budget for that event.
- No one took any photos. This has happened to me several times when I put myself in charge of taking photos.
- Having the administrator say something inappropriate (but true) because I did not prep him on what to say.

- Allowing residents to attend without having a prospect as a guest. (Then all residents with the canes and walkers will want to come to every marketing event.)
- Not having an ending time on the invitation, because they don't get to stay all night.
- Having the musicians play too long, because I never gave them a timeline (I graciously had to cut them off after they ended a musical piece).
- Not having door prizes in order to capture each guest's contact information.
- The worst blooper would be not having any new prospects. This blooper has never happened to me, thank goodness.

The purpose of having three to four unusual or interesting events per year is to attract new faces and resurrect people on your waiting list. If people believe your community is the same old thing day after day, there is no reason to visit it again because they know all about it. If they don't revisit it, they cannot picture themselves living there. Ohhh, so *that* is why occupancy is down. That's right! People need to visualize living in the community before they sell their home to move there.

Chapter 7
Never Say to the Customer…

This chapter is not just for the marketing team. It's for *everyone* in your organization. There are offensive words to seniors that need to be avoided. For everyone in your organization to earn a salary, it is dependent upon marketing to have full occupancy. Your words can affect jobs at your community. Your words can affect a sale. This is a big responsibility. Do not let a stumble with an offensive word or statement ruin a sale. What you say *to other staff* can become a habit and accidentally be said in front of the customer.

Remember that words either build value or take away value! What is your retirement community's biggest competition? No, it is not the community down the street. It is someone staying in their own home. From the moment someone drives in your parking lot until you say, "Looking forward to seeing you again," (note that I did not say, "good-bye"), it should be about building value and lifestyle that makes it worth giving up their home.

For the Health Care Services Background Team and All Staff

You are marketing a "community" not a "facility." (In this case, everyone who works there is marketing.) Who in their right mind would want to live in a "facility?" Would you? It sounds like an institution. It's a new century and the boomers are a prime target market. No one wants to live in a "facility" or be "put in a bed." It's a *community,* and if they ever need health services, it would be in a "private suite" in the health center (these are the most marketable and the highest value) or in a "semi-private suite." Don't call it "a bed."

It is a true statement that you can "admit" someone to health services, but they should never be admitted to "independent residential living." They "move into" that area. Someone may not need health services for ten or twenty years, so persuade them to "move in" first and you have plenty of time to "admit" them years later to a higher level of care.

They are "residents" not "patients." Never have I heard a health services staff say the word "diaper," but sometimes other staff does, so watch out for this. Diaper??! There goes Charlie Brown again, "Aghhhh!"

Tout your "rehab gym" to add value for short-term stays. Think about it. Would you want to tell your friends you're going to a "rehab gym" or to a "therapies room"? Add value by saying the rehab gym is for physical, occupational, and speech therapy or whatever you offer.

Most communities no longer have "wings." The new verbiage is "neighborhoods." If your community has not yet changed this language, I strongly encourage you to do so as part of a branding effort. Words can make a community sound aged or vibrant. Boomers want to live in a vibrant and healthy community.

The following term is a bit controversial and could depend on the competition in your market. In Seattle, the competition is mighty. There are many stand-alone communities offering two levels of care. If everyone refers to "health care" as "health services," then all the communities (even those with three and four levels of care) sound the same to the customer.

Tip: For the stand alones with two levels of care, continue referring to health services. It's an effective strategy against CCRCs with three or four levels of care.

Tip: For the CCRCs with four levels of care: Explain each of your lifestyle options to your customers. If they ever need future health care, it will be available in the community, such as "assisted living," "secured memory care" (always say "secured" if you have it), and "skilled care nursing." If someone's spouse (never use the person in front of you as the example) were recovering from a hip replacement and needed skilled care nursing, then that person would be an elevator ride away from the spouse. If you are Medicare certified then say so. It adds value.

Do not give the resident or prospective guest a taste of your own in-house alphabet soup. Are you guilty of saying "SNF," "AL," "MC," or "IL?" Never use these terms in front of the customer.

If you ever hear staff call it "AL" to a customer's face, then your whole team now needs to call it "assisted living" to support that team member who might accidentally say it to the customer again. I personally like to say "SNF" (pronounced sniff) in an e-mail or talking with colleagues, but ALWAYS say "skilled care nursing" to the customer.

Never Say to the Customer...

I believe almost everyone who curses or uses coarse language can turn it off in front of their parents, priest, or clergy member. Some people cannot. Know your own limits and those of your staff. Watch your alphabet soup language too!

Use health services words that add value and differentiate you from the competition!

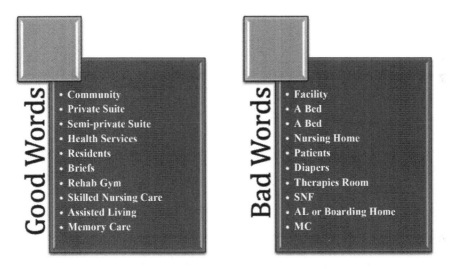

Good Words	Bad Words
• Community	• Facility
• Private Suite	• A Bed
• Semi-private Suite	• A Bed
• Health Services	• Nursing Home
• Residents	• Patients
• Briefs	• Diapers
• Rehab Gym	• Therapies Room
• Skilled Nursing Care	• SNF
• Assisted Living	• AL or Boarding Home
• Memory Care	• MC

For the Development, Construction, and Maintenance Teams and All Staff

Okay, so you already know to use "community" instead of "facility." Your next big no-no word is "unit." There is no bigger word in my vocabulary that ruins the value built by a marketing person than a construction or design person saying the word "unit" to the customer. Customers want to leave their beautiful homes and move to an apartment home. They do not want to move to a "unit." The proper value term to use would be "an apartment home." Teach this to all your front line staff.

Construction staff can really build value by discussing granite, tile, wood flooring, extra-large windows, washers, dryers, energy efficient appliance packages, green design features, energy savings, and quality construction. Prospective residents love to hear your decision to obtain LEED certification (Leadership in Energy and Environmental Design), because it can keep his or her monthly fees down with its heating and cooling efficiencies.

Project managers get paid the big bucks and should be "bilingual." They should have the ability to talk construction lingo with the contractors and sub-contractors, then turn on a switch and change their language to value-driven words if they are in the presence of customers.

For Those in Development

It's fantastic to have the construction project manager speak at marketing events. This builds value. People love the details about the NEW community building where they are going to move. Always include fun facts, such as how much dirt was excavated, how many trucks of concrete it took, the numbers of pilings, or some other fascinating fact. Give them teasers on when they can have a hard hat tour and see the inside of the community building themselves. They love this.

For the Operations Team

It's a "community" with "apartment homes." You can build value by saying "community spaces" versus "common spaces." Do you want to have "common space" in *your* home? Would you give up your own home to move to "a unit with common space?" No way! Refer to them as "beautiful community spaces" that are part of their home. They can access them twenty-four hours a day, for example by reading in the library at 2 a.m. or exercising in the health club without getting in a car and driving to the gym.

Here are more words that build value:

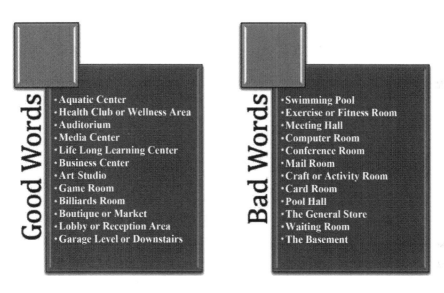

Good Words
- Aquatic Center
- Health Club or Wellness Area
- Auditorium
- Media Center
- Life Long Learning Center
- Business Center
- Art Studio
- Game Room
- Billiards Room
- Boutique or Market
- Lobby or Reception Area
- Garage Level or Downstairs

Bad Words
- Swimming Pool
- Exercise or Fitness Room
- Meeting Hall
- Computer Room
- Conference Room
- Mail Room
- Craft or Activity Room
- Card Room
- Pool Hall
- The General Store
- Waiting Room
- The Basement

The word "meal" has no value. "Meals" are served in the military (no offense and God bless our troops). Value words are "dinner," "lunch," "breakfast," "brunch," and "dining choices." These sound expensive, desirable, fun, classy, and enjoyable as in a restaurant experience.

Add value to your community by referring to "multiple dining venues," "restaurants," or "dining experiences." If all you have is a dining room and room service, then those are "multiple dining venues." Please note that I did not call it a "tray service" or "sick tray service to your room." Saying "room service deliveries to your apartment home" builds VALUE! It makes it sound like a fine hotel.

It adds value to build as much choice into dining as possible. This is an operations choice that can make or break marketing to the customer. For example: "Dinner is served between 5:30 and 8 p.m." (sounds flexible) vs. "the dinner seating is at 5 p.m. or 6 p.m." (sounds inflexible). Why be so rigid? It's all about choice for the active customers; boomers want flexible dining options.

For the Marketing Team and All Staff

There *is* such a thing as being too honest with the customer with statements such as:

- "You were on my list to call today."
- "You were on my schedule to be followed up with today."
- Telling the customer you will retain 10 percent of the entrance fee. Instead say, "The entrance fee is 90 percent refundable to your estate."
- NEVER EVER refer to *people* as "a sale!"

Please don't call them "prospects" in their presence or to their faces. They are all your "guests" or "future residents." Please note: The term "prospect" or "prospective guests" is meant for marketing and is only to be used in-house. In the *prospect's* presence the term to use is "guest." I might say, "Mrs. Jones, I have an appointment later with another 'guest' who is interested in this two-bedroom apartment home with the view of the park." Here are alternative terms: "prospective resident," "depositor," "charter member," "future resident," "wait list depositor," or "friend of a resident."

Yes...these are real examples that can really happen when working with prospective guests. Treat guests like gold. It's about building long-term relationships. They are real human beings who want preferential treatment. They want to feel that they are the most important people in the world. Give them *sincere* VIP treatment.

Phraseology of the Paperwork

When you are at the point to discuss the paperwork, refer to it as an "agreement" not a "contract." Never ask them to "sign the contract." Before they came today, someone probably told them not to sign anything. Instead your language should be: "Please put your okay there," or I love to say, "Your John Hancock goes right here." It's patriotic and EVERYONE knows what John Hancock signed.

Tip: If your community has pens with your logo on them, it is a nice gesture to present them with a pen here.

People have a real fear of being "SOLD." People love to "BUY!"

When prospective guests are considering your community as their future home, what runs through their minds? What small talk are you making while writing up the paperwork that could offend them so that they cancel later?

Let's consider a few examples of what may be running through the prospective guests' minds:

They should move in because they don't have kids:

- There is no one to take care of them as they age.
- The nurse at the community can be their advocate if they go to the hospital.
- They want to spend all their money now and don't care about refundable entrance fees.

They should move in because they do have kids:

- They are moving in so kids don't have to make decisions later to put them somewhere.
- They like the idea of a refundable entrance fee going to their kids or themselves when they leave the community.

These thoughts are all emotional connections that add value. While they are building value in their heads, don't detract from it by saying things like:

- "When you are dead or gone." Instead add some humor and say, "When you have left the building either vertically or horizontally." (They always laugh, and humor is great!)
- "The entrance fee is refundable to your kids." Instead say, "The entrance fee is refundable to your estate." (This is a good habit because it is sensitive to guests who have no kids or are estranged from them.)

What are the *residents saying* to their friends who are interested in being prospective residents?

How often have you heard a resident say:

- Inmates
- Facility
- Nursing home
- The home
- Unit
- A bed
- A room
- An institution
- The old folks home

Take time to gently reeducate residents at a resident council meeting or through a newsletter. Let them know that their friends may think that this wonderful retirement community is "the home" or "an institution." Tell them to invite their friends to see this beautiful community and to throw away their preconceived idea of "the home" their parents might have lived in for care. This is not your grandmother's retirement home. It's been built to attract boomers.

What are you calling your prospects? Hopefully you are not using *that* word! Especially to their faces! Never ever call anyone a "prospect!" Make a fun quiz for your staff with good phraseology versus bad. Hand out lots of small prizes for correct answers.

Chapter 8
Selling to Personalities

Are you selling to their personality type—or yours?

This is one of my favorite subjects. It's fun. There are so many personality tests out there, but they all tend to boil down to four categories. It works great to utilize this information for prospective guests, but it also works great on the boss, colleagues, spouse, family, kids, and friends.

From a marketing perspective, it's important to have a well-rounded tour or presentation that appeals to the generalities of all four personality types. To do this it's *essential* to have a discovery conversation in the early part of your meeting to determine what type of personality someone is. Then you fine-tune all of *your* strategies for *their* type of personality.

There are people who are combinations of personalities, but everyone has a predominant personality.

Here are a few discovery questions to help you determine someone's personality:

- Have you looked at any other retirement communities? What do you consider the most important feature or amenity?
- What is/was your field of expertise?

- What type of work did you do or are still currently doing?
- What are your favorite hobbies?
- How do you like spending your time?
- Do have any friends who live here?
- How did you find out about this community? (If it's a friend or family member, then explore this.)

First Personality Type – The Leader

- This senior customer is usually a retired CEO, business owner, or had some leadership capacity in his or her career.
- The customer is involved in groups that he or she still leads. (These can be fantastic referrals because people respect this leader.)
- You can picture this person becoming your new resident council president.
- This person prefers being in control of all situations.
- The leader may take charge of his or her own tour at your community and tell you what he or she wants to see.

Their strengths are a drive to succeed, willingness to take a leadership role, goal-oriented, and competitive. Their weaknesses can be a tendency to be controlling, bossy, impatient, not listening, because they think they already know they are right and tend to not be sensitive to others' feelings. (They just don't realize the feelings because they are so focused on succeeding.)

How to talk to and give a tour to a leader personality:

Do:

- Be the marketing expert that this person can rely on for accurate information.

- Talk *factually* about the community.
- Elaborate on how your community has succeeded in differentiating itself from its competitors.
- Share briefly about awards that your community has won. (This appeals to the prospect's competitive spirit.)
- Offer to give the prospect a copy of the audited financial report.
- Introduce him or her to people of power on the tour (residents who were former CEOs, the administrator, the chef, the human resources director, etc.).

The No-No's:
- Do not tell this prospect your life story or relate any personal stories.
- Let me repeat: Don't talk about yourself, positive though it may be.
- Don't be intimidated by this person's credentials.
- Be careful not to let this person push you around by creating his or her own order of the tour.
- When this person demands that you just show him or her an apartment (and spare the "sales pitch") don't do it. Sit in the lobby first and do your discovery. I usually say, "I will absolutely show you some apartments today, but I don't want to waste your time by showing you the wrong ones. Tell me, what prompted your visit today?"

Sales Implications

Once they make a decision to move to your community, leader personalities can be a great advocate for you as they are 100 percent sold to your community's concept and lifestyle. When they refer their friends, the friends already have a trust built in your community.

marketing2seniors.net

Complications

A spouse can be a completely different personality who needs to be treated according to another personality type. This requires expert discovery at the onset of your meeting with them to determine how you will work on appealing to two types of personalities at the same time. It also determines who the decision maker is. Note: The decision maker is usually the woman while leader personalities for current seniors tend to be men. As the boomers start to move in to retirement communities, there will be many more women leaders.

Let me share a common example:

A retired CEO comes on tour with his bride of fifty years. He peppers you with very specific questions to determine if you are a viable community for his consideration. The wife is quiet as the husband drives the conversation. I answer questions very factually (without the fluffy adjectives). Depending on the questions, I might sit with them for thirty minutes, including my discovery. If I can't answer a question, I ask permission to make a note of it and follow up with the answer in twenty-four hours. I always ask the wife a few questions, even if he frowns upon it, to build rapport with her. Once I have completed answering most of the questions (not all, because of time), we then begin the physical tour of the building. As we walk down the hall, I work on connecting the hot buttons of her personality, whether it's connectivity with friends who live in the building or appealing to her other interests.

 **Tip: The retired CEO will usually let his wife select the apartment home. He** *acts* **like he is the decision maker of everything. The reality is that once he determines that your community is a good value for the money then his wife will select a specific apartment to create their new home together.**

135

Second Personality Type – Analytical

- This senior customer is usually a retired CFO, accountant, financial planner, attorney, software engineer, librarian, or some type of introverted career person. (This is not always the case. For example, I am predominantly analytical but have the ability to be extroverted too.)
- His or her hobbies are usually reading, computers, and sometimes photography.
- This person will be very interested in your finance and budget committee.
- He or she is quiet and can be hard to open up during discovery.

This person's personality strengths tend to make him or her a perfectionist, organized, detail oriented, talented and creative in the arts, and sensitive to others' needs. This person's weaknesses are being a perfectionist, too analytical, moody, and not being the life of the party (possibly not talkative or not very social at the party).

Do:
- Be the marketing expert that this person can rely on for accurate information.
- Talk factually about your community.
- Tell this person about lifelong learning opportunities or photography classes that may interest him or her.
- Talk about the privacy of an apartment home. (This personality type recharges by being alone.)
- Detail how your community has succeeded in being financially strong during a tough economic time.
- Share the longevity of the organization.

- Talk about the transparency of the financial information (if you are permitted by your management).
- Offer a copy of the audited financial report.

The No-No's:
- Do not be Social Sally and tell this person your life story or any personal stories.
- Let me repeat: Don't talk about yourself, positive though it may be.
- Don't use a lot of descriptive adjectives. Keep sentences short and simple.
- Don't tell this person that everyone in the community will become a friend. It will scare him or her away.
- Be careful to not over-share about community groups or social activities (this is a delicate topic for this personality).

Sales Implications

Once they have analyzed your community to their satisfaction, analytical people will be a solid sale. Their very small circle of friends will want a tour. Secondary sales from analytical personality types are very common. Once this person is a depositor, his or her friends tend to have complete trust in your organization.

Tip: Analytical personality types love reading material. They will read every word of the brochure and website. Analytics want extra reading material before they commit and even after the sale is secure. Make sure to give them updated copies of the audited financial statements.

Complications

It's easy to scare off analytical personalities. They need to know they can live in a communal setting and still have privacy. It's important to emphasize that residents can enjoy the privacy of their own apartment home. When sharing the health club equipment, for example, emphasize, "There are times of day when it's busy and other times when only a single resident is using the equipment." Analytical personalities do not want to feel that they will be pounced on by other residents every time they exit their apartment.

Third Personality Type – The Social Butterfly

- This personality tends to be an extrovert, female (not always), who already knows some of your residents.
- She is very well connected in social clubs in your city.
- She may be a snowbird (traveling to warm climates in the winter) with social connectivity in another state as well.
- She is an excellent referral source.
- The social butterfly is always the life of the party and people love being her friend.
- This person's hobbies are bridge, cards, board games, social clubs, coffee groups, theater groups, travel groups, and anything that's considered fun.

Social butterflies' strengths are being fun-loving, animated, optimistic, and excited about life. Their weaknesses can be talking too much, forgetful, late to appointments, undisciplined, and insecure with their decisions.

Do:
- Tell them right up front that the tour will be fun. They will be thrilled and smile.
- Let them know how they can connect and socialize within your community. Share anecdotes on how they can do this.
- Talk about the movies, describe outings, share the latest resident party, and be very descriptive with enthusiasm.
- Show them photos of events your community has produced.
- Let them know they will never have to eat alone.
- Tell them a couple of personal stories; they *do* want to know about you! (Be careful! Wasting valuable time talking about yourself will not sell the community. Just say enough to connect and build a relationship with this personality.)
- Tell them interesting anecdotes about other residents.
- Describe holiday festivities.
- Introduce them to other residents on the tour.

The No-No's:
- Do not be Boring Brad.
- If you are too factual or boring, you can scare off this type of person.
- Don't offer a financial report. They don't care.
- Do not make them feel bad for being late to the appointment. (Of course, you should never make anyone feel bad about this, but this personality is particularly sensitive.)

Sales Implications

It's difficult to have this personality commit to a tour. They often cancel two to four times because of social obligations that take precedence. Once they do select an apartment, they may cancel a week later. It's difficult for them to make a decision and follow through on the decision. When they sell their home, they feel that they are giving up all their neighborhood friendships. Any friend can sway them to change their commitment to move to your community with just one conversation or comment.

 **Tip: Have a resident they know invite them to lunch, which will solidify setting an appointment or possibly even the sale for you. Social butterflies desire a lot of attention, so keep following up with them and they will move in to be in proximity with old acquaintances or to develop new friendships.**

Complications

If they have friends at two different competing senior communities, it's difficult for them to make a decision.

Children of social butterflies tend to look out for them. Give the analytical or leader children the financial information, but don't burden the social butterflies with it. It will become too much for them and they will pull out because it's no longer fun. The kids will not care because they think they are protecting their parents.

Opposites do attract, therefore social butterflies are usually married to a leader personality. Keep a balance of the do's and don'ts from both categories.

Fourth Personality – Peacemakers

- This personality tends to be a people pleaser, hard worker, quiet, calm, and relaxed.
- Peacemakers want to avoid conflict.
- Peacemakers will set up a tour when you call them, but never really make a decision to move forward.
- They are excellent volunteers and will work hard for a cause or leader they believe in.

Their strengths are loyalty, patience, compassion toward others, easy-going, and being a great mediator in controversy. Their weaknesses are avoiding confrontation (which is sometimes avoiding you the salesperson), passive, unmotivated, and letting other people push them around (to avoid conflict).

Do:
- Find out who their friends are in the community. They are very loyal to their friends.
- A lot of discovery with this person to identify hot buttons.
- Talk about the secure feeling of being a part of the community, in case anything were to ever happen.
- Be very respectful of this personality. (Be respectful of all, but this personality thrives on it.)
- Continuously reassure them that they are making the right decision.
- Share how supportive the residents are to their neighbors in and outside the building.

The No-No's:

- Do not be Pushy Paul.
- Don't ask them to lead a resident committee (they would hate it).
- Never be critical of any resident, policy, or competitors.
- Avoid changing the salesperson (since they have built loyalty with the first one).
- Don't discuss any conflicts in the community or surrounding neighborhood or anything regarding politics.

Sales Implications

These can be your hardest sales to secure. I suggest having their analytical accountant friend or leader CEO friend reassure them that moving to your community is the best choice for their future.

 **Tip: Keep following up with peacemaker personalities. At some point, they will understand that you are committed (loyal) to their best interests. This trust can build a bond that entices them to make a commitment and select an apartment. Be patient, as it can take a year or more.**

Complications

You keep following up with them and can't understand why they won't move forward. These personality types can be pushed around, but they are often indecisive and won't ever make a decision.

Dominant Personality Traits

Some people seem to have a little of all four personality types wrapped up together but one is always dominant. Are they more extroverted (the leader and social butterfly personality types) or introverted (the analytical and peacemaker personality types)? Extroverted people recharge being with other people. Introverted personalities recharge all alone.

The Personalities of Marketing Staff

Let's take a moment to determine how our own personalities can affect our sales.

Leader Salespeople
- Sell the results of living in the community (benefits)
- Close sales often
- Have a high activity level
- Lack compassion

Analytical Salespeople
- Sell the logic of the move
- Are well prepared
- Have great follow up
- Tend to lack emotional appeals

Social Butterfly Salespeople
- Sell connecting to others in the retirement community
- Share enthusiasm of the community
- Excellent at building relationships instantly
- Lacking in follow ups

Peacemaker Salespeople

- Sell the support and service of the community
- Give reliable service
- Empathetic to the customer
- Lack closing urgency

What is Your Personality Type?

Have you determined your personality type? There is no perfect personality. Every person has his or her own unique strengths and weaknesses. Build on your own strengths and minimize your weaknesses to the best of your ability. Take a test or ask a trusted friend to help determine your strengths and weaknesses.

I enjoy all personalities, but my favorites to sell to are CFOs, accountants, and attorneys. That's because the analytical persona is my most predominant personality and I can relate to these people. It's really fun to study personalities on an ongoing basis. Sometimes a peacemaker personality can put me to sleep because he or she is so boring to my personality type. (Others are lovely people who are sweet and kind.) Then a social butterfly comes in and I have a ball with him or her and wake right up.

My final thought to share on this subject is that staff, family members, and possibly even you can wear a masked personality at times. When I met my husband, I originally thought he had an extroverted personality (his mask) when he is actually an introverted peacemaker. Some people in sales have perfected eliminating the weaknesses of their personality at work. It's amazing but true.

Chapter 9
Hard or Soft Closing?

Can you wrestle someone to the ground so he or she will select an apartment? How about brow-beating people into submission by telling them they are Stupid Stanley or Dopey Dora if they don't go ahead today? Okay, I am overdramatizing what some managers imply the marketers should do. If we treat people like Pushy Patty, they'll never want to come back. It's exponentially worse when they tell their friends about their horrible experience at your community when they're with a gathering of fellow seniors.

Great closing is an art. It is one of the most fulfilling, exciting, exhilarating, and challenging aspects of my personal career. Simply put, I love it. I encourage everyone to keep challenging themselves by reading books (Congratulations! You're obviously doing that!) and listening to tapes on this subject.

 **Tip: Prospective residents can sense if you are Sammy Sales or if you have their best interests at heart. Do you? Many residents I have helped to select an apartment hug me on sight. They often lower their voices and say, "Diane, thank you for helping us get the best apartment in the whole building. We love it." I smile at them and softly say, "I know it's the best and I am glad you**

love it." What a feeling to build a relationship that can help improve somebody's life forever! I believe I am making a positive difference and that each couple or single will have a better life in the community than in their own home. They know by my words, actions, and nonverbal communications that I want what is truly best for them.

How do you accomplish this? First of all, it's important to have a great attitude and be prepared with as much information about the prospective resident as possible. (See "Attitude Toward Occupancy – Turn Your Change into Dollars" and "Do you have Proactive Marketing or Reactive Marketing" chapters in this book.) Secondly, have an end goal for the appointment. Possible end goals are either the person making a deposit or selecting an apartment to move into.

What should you take on your appointment? Enclose all the possible paperwork needed in a leather portfolio.

When the appointment was set over the phone, the prospective guests probably stated that they were never going to buy anything. I love it when they say this; it usually means it's a sale. It's a protection mechanism that people say hoping it will stop them from buying or ensure they're getting a good deal. Now you are toward the end of the sale and they have just decided to select an apartment. You could still lose the sale. How? When you leave them to go get the paperwork or pen, they could talk themselves out of it. Therefore you must be totally prepared. Here is what to bring on every appointment regardless of what they told you on telephone:

Hard or Soft Closing?

- The wait list application
- Depositor application and any additional forms
- Floor plans
- Two pens—one for you and one for them. (Plus it's a back-up in case you run out of ink.)
- Note pad to take notes
- Anything else?

 **Tip: I like to give them a pen at the beginning of a question and answer meeting (usually a second or third look). It's advertising for the community with the logo on it. It encourages them to take notes. It subtly gets them in the mindset to put their "okay" (signature) on a residency agreement.**

Your scheduled appointment has just arrived. When does the closing start?

It starts at the beginning of your appointment. In some rare circumstances people ask before the appointment is halfway over, "What is available now?" If you say, "We will cover that later," you just lost the sale. This chapter will focus on being a good listener and letting them buy at their own pace.

Opening is as important as closing.

The customer's first impression is your professionalism and your *genuine* friendliness. This sets the tone for the customer to listen *to* you. Think of some first lines you use when greeting the customer.

Here are a few examples:

- "Welcome, I'm glad you're here." (Say this as you shake hands.)
- "Good afternoon, I'm Diane Masson, and I'm here to serve you today."
- "Welcome to (give the name of our community). I'm glad you're here."
- "Welcome! I've been looking forward to giving you a tour (or showing you our community) today."
- "It's great to see you again, Mr. and Mrs. Smith. Let's take a moment to be seated over here."

Initial greetings should convey warmth, sincerity, energy, and a desire to help them as people deserving to be treated with dignity. Make sure you shake hands with just the right amount of firmness. Some people have arthritis, so be careful, but don't give a limp noodle handshake either.

Remember:

- *You* **set the tone for the sales appointment.**
- **It's *your* attitude.**
- **It's *your* level of enthusiasm.**
- **It's *your* belief in your community being the best.**

Invite them to sit back down, if they just stood up to greet you. Make introductions all around and memorize all the names and relationships. Your next few minutes are critical to take the pressure off them and to help them relax. Let them know that your goal is to answer all their questions and send them home with the information they need to know about your community.

Hard or Soft Closing?

It's all about building a relationship from the minute they walk in the door. Some people call it discovery. It's asking open-ended questions to find out the prospective resident's situation today.

What are some of your favorite phrases to get people to open up to you?

Opening questions:

- What prompted your visit with us today?
- What are you looking for in your next home?
- What is important to you?
- Do you have friends who live here?
- What are your favorite hobbies?
- Do you have family living in the area?
- What does your family think about your being here? The answer to this is always fascinating – Either:
  - o The kids don't know – "It's none of their business and I don't want to be a burden to them" or
  - o The kids pushed them to come in because they are worried. (Find out why the kids are worried.)

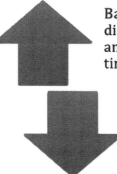

Balanced Bradley asks discovery questions and listens 75% of the time = sale.

Babbling Bella shares her own life story, talking the majority of time = no sale.

The most effective salespeople spend their time on an appointment:

- **25 percent questioning**
- **75 percent listening**

Are you listening more than talking? Remember, you have two ears and one mouth.

If you spoke with them on the phone, bring up those discoveries again to see if they hold true in person. For example, suppose they said that they have already visited two retirement communities. After the initial greeting and opening questions, commend them on their research efforts in studying those other communities. Find out if they have friends at them and if their friends are settled in and satisfied. Upon exploration, they reveal that their friends are often unhappy or critical of your competitor. When you give the tour later, make sure to accentuate your competitor's weaknesses as your strengths—without saying one bad word about the competition.

Hot Buttons

During discovery, your goal is to flesh out their hot buttons without making them feel grilled by you. The majority of hot buttons (95 percent) are concerned with helping arrange health care for a close relative or friend. In other words, they discuss, "Putting Mom in a nursing home." Or they had an emergency situation with a friend who was forced to select an undesirable nursing home because it was all that was available. These situations always left the one needing care without a choice.

Who wants to be in a situation where they don't have control? Your prospects don't want their kids or family members to "put them somewhere." They want to make their own decisions while they can. Many people have felt a huge responsibility in caring for a parent and don't want to burden their own children someday. This is why they came to your community today. It has zero to do with real estate (the apartment size and view) and everything to do with this hot button.

Tip: Don't exploit a hot button. Murmur a kind affirmation and encourage them to expound on it further. If it takes them ten minutes or longer to share the hot button, sing alleluia inside your head. Without their knowing it, they are creating an emotional connection to your community and urgency for themselves. Listen carefully; you officially have my permission to bring it up again toward the end of the appointment. If you use the hot button at the right time, in the right way (with their best interest at heart), the sale is closed.

People love to buy! People hate to be sold!

Discovery captures why they are there. Ask them why they came. "What prompted your visit today?" Many times people say to me, "Oh, Diane, I love my home with its 180-degree view of the water. I could never leave it." Don't be afraid of this! Welcome their sharing about their beautiful home. Never interrupt them while they expound on their home. I have heard salespeople say, "Well, this is better!" Don't fight with the customer. When they are done, I simply say, "Your home sounds wonderful (ideal or perfect). What brought you here today?" Whatever comes out of their mouths next is the *real* reason. Make a note of it in your brain. They might say:

- "Well, I am not getting any younger and I know I'll need help someday."
- "Several of my friends have Alzheimer's (or some type of health challenge)."
- "My kids are worried about me."
- "I can't take care of my home (or yard) like I used to, it's too big and I can't do stairs anymore."

Again, murmur sympathy and let them expound on this emotional decision. If you focus on supporting them through their fears, they will sell themselves. Making the difference with discovery results in no pushy hard sell. If you are just a tour guide and race people through the building, it accomplishes nothing.

This chapter works hand in hand with an earlier chapter entitled *Building Value for Your Community – Giving a Wow Experience*. Please refer to it. Are you telling stories and painting the lifestyle picture for them or just saying, "This is the meeting hall."?

If your visitors already had a tour a month or more ago, briefly build value for areas of the community that had *value for them* in a previous tour. Be entertaining. Have at least one appropriate joke, humorous comment, or anecdote. Are you building the "wow factor" into your tours? Several of my worst tours were when one of my visitors went to sleep. At first it's insulting, but then I realized that I had better be more exciting and vary my voice tones by getting louder and softer. Several months later, I found out that one of my sleeping spouses (on a tour) passed away. He was tuckered out toward the end of his life and slept a lot, so it was not a case of my being a Dull Diane and putting him to sleep. But it was still a good lesson for me.

Objections

It does not matter where our retirement communities are located in the country; we all have the same objections. What is the number one objection? That's right: "I want to think about it." Objections are one of two things. Either something we failed to cover during our time (discovery and tour) with them or they simply need more information.

Tip: If you wait until the end of your time together to cover objections, then you are battling the prospective resident and creating a stressful sales experience by being a Stressful Sally. You can cover objections before they become an objection by using examples of past tour experiences. It's the "friend approach" and it's very effective. I suggest role-playing responses with the "friend approach" for the top four or five objections you will typically hear.

For example you know through your discovery:

- The couple has a 3000-square-foot (or larger) home.
- They want to wait about six months before selling their home.
- Several years ago the wife had to find a nursing facility for her mom in an emergency situation.

I proceed to share a story about some other residents who moved in recently and why. I might say, "I know you want a two bedroom that is X square feet with a view of X. You've also indicated to me that you would like to wait about six months before selling your home. My suggestion is to consider what some other residents did who just moved in. (Pause here for effect and trust me, they *will* be listening.) When they found the perfect apartment for them, they put a deposit on it and listed their home. It ended up taking about six months to sell their home. They said they were glad to take advantage of the home market when it was hot. They said it was good to strike while the iron is hot. They had some friends who waited until everything was perfect to sell, and then it took a lot longer to sell their home. Now they are happy in their perfect apartment home. Coincidentally, Mary had a sudden need for the health center on a temporary basis. She said it was great when her husband could just come downstairs to visit her. No one ever knows when they might need the health center. I would love for you to meet them. They are a wonderful couple."

Now shut up and wait to see what they say. If the salesperson speaks at this time, the sale will be lost.

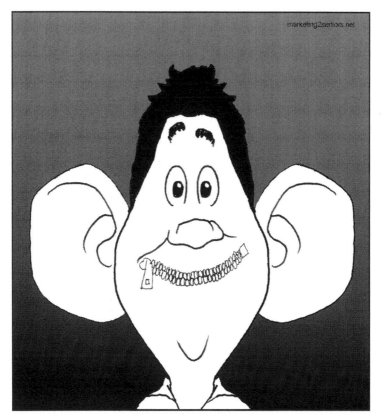

If we do a good job in discovery, we should be able to cover the majority of objections before they come up. Hearing the same objection at the end of every presentation is a good indication that there is something you're not covering in your time with prospective guests. Practice in your head and role-play with others to improve these talking points in preparation for your next encounter with a prospective resident.

Let's start with recognizing closing questions that they may ask you. The questions can come in the beginning, the middle, or the end of your presentation. When they ask you a question, never answer with a simple "yes "or "no." It's good to answer with a clarifying question that allows more discoveries as to their needs or wants. Your strategic question can often turn into an early close and result in the sale.

Recognizing Buying Questions

For example, if they ask, "Is this apartment available?" You ask, "What is your time frame for moving in?" The answer given is *very* telling. They might say, "Well, I have to sell my home first." This indicates they want to buy it! You just have to walk them through the steps on how to make it a reality.

More Buying Questions

- Asking about availability of a certain apartment.
- What is the time frame required to move into this apartment?
- They want something repeated.
- Wanting to know about rates, price, or affordability.
- Asking about the quality or levels of health care that are offered is a great sign.
- Wanting to see the model apartment.
- Asking what the other residents are like.
- Comparing your community with the competition. This means they are doing their homework and are interested.

They may say, "How much money would I have to put down to hold it?" This is not a sale until you walk them through all the steps. But it's darned close!

Hard or Soft Closing?

Types of Closes

- The best close in the world, and one of my personal favorites, is, "The Either/Or Close."
  - o Say, "So are you thinking a three- **or** four-month time frame to move in will work for you?" Then shut up. If you say one word before they respond, they will go home and think about it. Have your paperwork ready and write it up.
  - o For assisted living say, "Gosh, I know you're thinking six months away, but when you come back in six months, I don't know what the wait will be then. I suggest you consider taking advantage of the choices now. Do you prefer the one-bedroom with the courtyard view **or** the one facing morning sun?"
- "The Sweet Close"
  - o When they first walk in the door I let them know I'm here to help and be at their service. I want to have a long-term relationship with them as they explore their choices and have some fun today.
  - o It puts people at ease, so it's no big deal when they give a buying signal to go right into a close—like "The Either/Or Close."
- "The Puppy Dog Close"
  - o It's giving people a test drive before they make a decision. We are not used car salespeople, so how can we do this?
  - o Offer them an overnight stay, a lunch, or a dinner to experience what it's really like to live in the community.
- "The Discovery Close"
  - o Find out what they like best and least. What at your community is most important to them? What at your

community is not available in their home? Do they have friends living at the community?

- o Take what you learned in discovery and turn it into an "Either/Or Close."
- o For example: You learned she hates to eat alone now that her husband is gone. I would say, "Do you enjoy cooking for yourself **or** do you like the idea of having dinner in the dining room almost every night?"
- "The Take it Away Close"
  - o This is also known as the urgency close and has lots of variations.
  - o Say, "We've had a tremendous response lately and this is my only apartment like this. I have more appointments scheduled for this week and I expect this apartment to be taken next." Then shut up!

Make Urgency!

Okay, you've done everything right but they have no urgency to move in now. Sell the waiting list and create urgency for it. In your head you know that someone might be able to walk in today and buy an apartment—so what! One to five years from now, there may be a big wait for a one- or two-bedroom apartment (remember the boomers are aging). Be their friend and say, "I would feel bad if you came back in five years and expected to move in right away. It's very unusual that we have openings right now. It would be in your best interest to get on the wait list now. What if your situation changed suddenly with a health concern and you wanted to move in immediately or in one year? People on the waiting list always have priority." Then shut up!

Your wait list deposit should be coming in the mail if they don't give it to you that day. Again, it's all about emotional connections. A month later, they may say, "Why did we get on that retirement community's wait list? Oh yeah, Diane said it was a plan for our future." One year later when one of them has a health scare, who will they go to first—you or your competitor? You—because you cared enough to get them on the waiting list when they were not in an emergency situation.

"The No Close Close" if it's not an immediate sale.

Take what you learned from discovery and graciously end the appointment. Go back to your office and input detailed notes into your database. Always type in your next strategy and schedule the call. For example, type *Call Mrs. Smith's resident friend and have her invite them to dinner.* This will help the prospective residents experience the community, enjoy the food, and have connectivity with their friend. The friend will sell the community. Then call the resident the next day. (Residents get pretty excited about helping and will immediately call your guest. Caution: If they call the same day as your tour, it is too soon and too pushy.) Find out when the dinner is scheduled and then put it on your calendar to stop by their table and say hello. It's vital to call them the day after the dinner, when their emotion is still high from connecting with their friend. This technique has been a real winner for me to increase occupancy.

There are two philosophies in developing priority deposits for developing new senior housing.

One philosophy is to build a long-term waiting list or priority list for the "blue sky" community. The general idea is to amass hundreds of families that will someday want to move into this new community. When you make the announcement that it's time to select apartments, a certain percentage will go to the next level of committing with a 10 percent (or more depending on the state) deposit down. The rest will move into the community in two to ten years.

The other philosophy is to create a priority group to fill the building immediately. When it's time to take people to the conversion step of selecting an apartment and putting a larger deposit down, it's either make a commitment or they are off the list. This philosophy finds the immediate "cream of the crop" and discards Procrastinators Pete and Paula. The advantage is that your time is focused 100 percent on people who want to move in now. The disadvantage is that while your building is being built, a sudden health challenge can prompt a Procrastinator Pete or Paula to move now. Don't discard great future leads that can fill your building in future years.

Keep perfecting your closing techniques! Whether the end of your appointment results in a sale or not, analyze all aspects outlined in this chapter to see how you can improve yourself for the future.

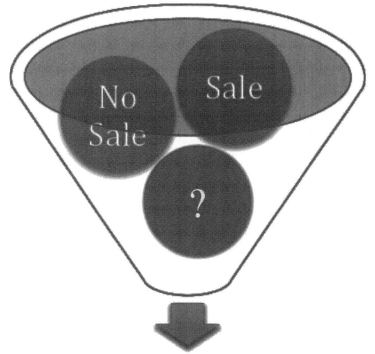

Critique yourself, so you can improve yourself for next time!

First, let's discuss what to do at the end of a sale, buttoning the sale up and analyzing what you did right!

I always ask the newly signed resident-to-be, "Why did you select an apartment? What is your number one reason for deciding to go ahead today?" Ask the same question to both spouses if it's a couple. Whatever they say, it's crucial to memorize it and put it in your database. If the depositor ever considers canceling the sale in the future (because it's too hard to sell their home, for example), it's vital to have this bit of information. Their answer will tell you what you did right in your presentation. Keep doing it. Usually the answer has to do with health care or planning for their future. If the answer is only about the apartment home, they may not be emotionally connected and the sale may not stick.

Buttoning up the sale is crucial to solidify the future move-in. How do you do this? After a salesperson writes up the paperwork, he or she can start to ramble. I have heard "Talking Too Much Tommy" start sharing personal information. Please don't get nervous and blow your sale. Remember, it's all about the customers until they walk out the door. I want the final statements in their heads to be orchestrated by me, and as they drive home, these words are the ones replaying in their heads.

The critical statements to be replayed in their heads need to be in general reference to their hot button and confirm that they have emotionally made the right decision.

I might say:

"Congratulations on having a plan for your future now."

"You never have to worry about your kids putting you some place; you've made your own decision for your future."

"This is a wonderful gift for your children so they don't have to make all the decisions that you had to for your parents."

"I'm glad we finally found the right apartment for you. Now you can sleep soundly knowing you have a solid plan for your future."

Hard or Soft Closing?

"Now you can go to sleep peacefully knowing there are no grey areas in your future."

"No matter what happens in the future, you will have priority access to great quality health services. I'm glad we found a floor plan that suits your lifestyle."

Not every appointment has great results.

If their final statement to me is, "Diane, you are a great salesperson," I think, "uh-oh!" It's a barometer that just told me I am off track. I will immediately go back to my desk and critique myself so that statement is not said to me next time. I consider customers saying this to be an insult. It meant that they did not feel a connection with me and that I was not truly looking out for their best interests. Upon reflection, I usually find that I hurried through or missed a step at the beginning of the appointment.

Great salespeople understand that closing takes persistence—either in scheduling the initial appointment or using multiple closes over multiple appointments. Study the chapter on personalities and understand why some people make quick decisions and others agonize over saying "yes." Some people can't even make a decision unless they have a friend or family member supporting them. Every prospective resident is unique, and they all need your expertise to strategically make them feel they are selecting their new home and not being sold. Treat them with individualized care.

Building the Community—One Relationship at a Time

Remember to build discovery with prospective residents to understand their needs and wants. Then it's easy to have the grace and compassion to have *their* best interests at heart. Build emotional connections throughout your presentation and tour (it's not just real estate). Recognize buying questions and test early "Either/Or Closes." Cover objections before they happen by being their friend and giving examples. If all else fails, create urgency for the wait list or use "The No Close Close" to increase occupancy.

Chapter 10
Internal Customers –
no need to worry about
them, right? Wrong!

Do you consider internal customers a key component to your success? They are, big time. Any internal customer (staff and residents) can affect a sale for marketing. How do you treat them on a *daily* basis? Do you take the time to teach them how to respond appropriately in front of a potential resident? Even if staff is off duty, they can influence potential customers either negatively or positively. Do they feel they are a valuable contributor to each sale?

The Marketing and Maintenance Relationship

I can still remember my first day on the job in senior housing. I was the new marketing director for a CCRC with two hundred independent apartment homes. The outgoing marketing director was to train me for one week. My excitement walking into her office quickly changed to discomfort as I witnessed a confrontation between her and the maintenance supervisor. The marketing director treated the maintenance supervisor like an unworthy animal or a dog. I was shocked and appalled.

As the week of training progressed, I learned that the confrontation I saw was just part of their ongoing "no collaboration" relationship. The marketing director complained to me, "I don't know why maintenance is so difficult all the time."

My first order of business after the outgoing marketing director left was to establish my own relationship with the maintenance supervisor. It started out tenuous at best. He had been treated like dirt for so long that he expected me to do the same. Instead, I made it a daily goal to either sincerely compliment some component of his work or tell him how much I appreciated working with someone with his skill set. Within a couple of weeks, we were friendly co-workers.

When I had my first marketing event several months later, the maintenance supervisor went beyond the call of duty to give me great service. To my delight and utter amazement, he brought a truck to help me load my equipment used at the event. I never even asked; he just volunteered to be helpful. I followed up this wonderful encounter with a note to his boss expounding on his helpfulness.

The next day the maintenance supervisor came into my office with tears in his eyes to thank me for writing a note to his boss.

Any senior community usually has a team to handle renovations that includes marketing and maintenance. Having healthy tension is normal. Marketing wants the newly renovated apartment perfect for the next customer as fast as possible. Maintenance wants to keep operational costs down and has limited working hours to perform the renovation. Tension arises when the normal number of apartment homes turning over doubles, triples, or quadruples.

One month, I had twelve apartment renovations that needed to be completed for twelve sales. This was quadruple the normal monthly amount. It was not possible for one human being to solely perform the renovations. The maintenance supervisor wanted to do it all. He was angry that we had not spaced out the move-ins, so he had to do all the maintenance himself. But I had to gently let him know how important each of those monthly fees was to the operating budget. Then I shared the stories of several desperate residents moving in because their homes were sold. I explained, "This is a very unusual month, so let's you and I (teamwork) come up with a solution that works and take it to the administrator." He agreed, and we ended up hiring outside painters and bringing on an assistant for him to complete all the renovations as scheduled. Everyone was happy and he and I patted ourselves on the backs for a job well done.

The Marketing and Environmental Services (Housekeeping) Relationship

In my experience, housekeepers typically don't have a lot of self-esteem. They are grateful for a job and some don't speak English very well. To me, this profession is invaluable to marketing. When my prospective guest stops in the community's restroom or when I walk a couple down the hall all I want them to see and smell is cleanliness. This aspect of operations is vital to marketing. It can make or break a one-on-one meeting, a presentation, or a major marketing event.

In each community, I learn the name of every housekeeper and greet him or her *by name* in every encounter, whether it's in the elevator or walking down the hall with guests. At first, there is always the look of surprise in being recognized by me. This is quickly followed with a smile of pleasure lighting up the whole face. I take great joy in watching their self-esteem grow over time.

Before a marketing event that entails prospective residents visiting every community space and public restroom in the building, I always have a meeting with the environmental supervisor (housekeeping). It's important to do this long before the event to give them planning and scheduling time. I share the importance of the event and how their team will have a major impact on a successful outcome.

We talk about how important cleanliness is to the customer. "How long does it take to vacuum the entire building?" I might ask. Then I add, "Please tell your team how much I value the vacuuming of the halls because I've noted they're always spotless when I take guests through." I continue, "Some people consider cleaning toilets unimportant, but I don't. I appreciate the attention to detail of your staff." Then we discuss who will check on the restrooms *during* the event to make sure the toilet paper, paper towels, and soap are plentiful.

Tip: After the event is over, I sincerely and enthusiastically share how vital the role of housekeeping was to people making a decision to get on the waiting list or become a depositor by selecting an apartment. They are blown away when I talk about individual sale results and the impact of the housekeeping team on those results. A thank you note (not an e-mail) is written to the supervisor with an e-mail going to their boss. I like to mention the staff members by name who were involved during the event.

Several times I have had housekeepers approach my desk with trepidation to thank me for writing a note to their supervisor on their excellent attention to detail. They can't believe that I would trouble myself to write a note to their supervisor. Many consider the marketing department the "elite" and themselves as "lowly workers." I treat the supervisor as an equal to the marketing director and each of their staff members as valuable contributors to each and every sale.

Once, during a tour, a prospective resident vomited in a hallway. It was a horrible experience. This person was embarrassed but wanted to continue the tour. I knew that I had to let housekeeping know so it would not absorb into the carpet. It was my responsibility since this was my customer and I wanted to clean it up, yet I was in a quandary because the customer needed immediate attention as well. On my way to get the environmental supervisor, I ran into a housekeeper at the elevator. I told her what happened and asked if she could help me. She immediately responded, "Of course! Don't worry." Later the housekeeper came to my office to let me know all was well. After I thanked her a hundred times, I wrote a letter to her supervisor and yet another note to the executive director to recognize this housekeeper's cheerful helpfulness during an embarrassing moment for the customer. All this transpired seamlessly because of the relationship of respect I built with housekeepers over time.

Marketing and the Chef Relationship

The chef is always a vital creative force in the retirement community. When he or she comes out to greet the guests in that white coat and chef hat after preparing excellent entrée selections, it is always impressive. The chef usually has a very big ego and loves recognition. My personal experience is: the better the cuisine, the bigger the ego. Make it a point to be your chef's friend.

Good chefs love marketing events. It's an opportunity for them to shine in the limelight and get some well-deserved attention. When I meet with a chef several months before an event, I share the marketing end goals (a great experience in the community that leads to deposits and move-ins). I invite the chef to create a menu within my budget for the event. Typically modifications are needed depending on the venue requirements, such as renaming the themed food selections, no pork, no nuts, or all finger foods (no fork required). This process can take a week or two depending on the chef, so plan ahead.

Tip: While the event is in progress, I love to recognize the chef from the podium and thank him or her for the lovely cuisine that everyone is about to enjoy. If it's appropriate for the event and if the chef is comfortable speaking publicly, I let him or her explain how the food has been prepared for them—describing the themed selections. When chefs speak of local vegetables, organic anything, or the sauces for the entrée, the audience becomes putty in their hands. Guests are usually drooling by the time the chef is done speaking, and this adds VALUE, VALUE and more VALUE.

It has been my pleasure to work with a chef who regularly greeted the future resident while we were having lunch. Many prospective residents have special dietary needs that come up while you are lunching together discussing which apartment home they will select. When the chef graces our table wearing that white coat and asks the prospective residents if they have any questions—wow! Most people are amazed that the chef took the time to speak with them, because the chef is the authority on food quality, preparation, and fine dining. The chef is always one of my favorite people in the community.

Marketing and Dining Staff Relationship

The residents love "the kids" (the dining staff). They never wanted to live with a bunch of old people, so they thoroughly enjoy interacting with the wait staff while dining. Depending on the community's location and proximity to schools, the staff is either predominantly high school or college students. It's always a gift to have committed staff who work in the dining room for four or more years.

The marketing department does not always know all the dining staff. Many servers work part-time as they are going to school. As their scheduled workday often begins at 5 p.m., the marketing person's day is usually concluding. So it's a good idea to keep your ears open around residents to find out who their favorite servers might be. These "favorites" might be the best ones to be serving at your next event.

After one marketing event that highlights food, you will have an opinion on the quality of the wait staff. The servers might be great at working with the residents but don't have the initiative to refill the buffet during the event or pass through the guests again with a fresh pot of coffee or tea.

Tip: My goal is to have one dining person responsible during the event. He or she is my "go to" person if anything happens while the guests are there. Maybe you just had a performance in your auditorium and now you are hosting two hundred guests with hors d'oeuvres and wines or a lovely luncheon. Now the marketer is working the room, greeting each person, and someone asks for more champagne. Or you notice that someone made a mess at the buffet table and dripped the salad dressing all over the

fluffed linen. Your "go to" person can correct these items immediately with a smile. That person should know where to find more linen to correct the spill and ask one of the servers (who might be in the kitchen gabbing to a young friend) to pour more champagne.

It is a plus and a minus to having a young wait staff. The plus is that their energy and youth usually outweigh their lack of anticipating serving needs and talking with co-workers. If possible, I request a meeting with key servers before a big event and let them know how vital their role will be to the success of the event. Some will care and be excellent servers and a few may only go through the minimum motions to be considered "working."

It has been my pleasure to write letters of recommendation for some servers as they are moving into their careers and higher schooling. Find the gems and request them for your next marketing event.

Marketing and Health Services Relationship

Health services have the vital role of caring for residents who are no longer 100 percent independent. It is never glamorous taking care of residents' bodily functions such as toileting or caring for grumpy people in pain. Their reputation as caregivers, response to call lights, and survey results are all of interest to independent prospective residents.

Make it a point to stay connected. My preferred way is by lunching with the health care administrator or director of nursing once a month. You can then get a pulse on what is currently happening. Be an encourager and let the administrator know what a critical role he or she plays in every independent sale. Ask him or her to share this with the health care team. Learn winning outcome health care stories that you can share with your marketing team.

If appropriate, invite the health services director to be a speaker at an upcoming marketing event. This adds credibility and value. The topic would be determined by marketing and perceived as valuable to prospective residents. Obviously the story or topic would have to comply with HIPAA and other regulations. Often residents, if asked, are willing to let their stories be shared. Great stories would be something like a full recovery from a hip or knee replacement.

When you hear great stories from recovered residents, tout them to the health services workers. Smile and tell them how much they are appreciated when you pass them while walking down the hall or in the elevator. Watch them glow with pride.

Marketing and the Residents Relationship

On the cautionary side, residents can have the most *inappropriate* stories come out of their mouths at an inopportune time—such as while you are giving a tour to a prospective resident. Honestly, they don't want to sabotage the marketing efforts; they may just be a natural Negative Nellie or Whining Willy.

One time I had closed a sale on a lovely apartment home and the prospective resident wanted to meet other residents and have dinner in the dining room. The next day I had a phone call from a now distraught depositor. She told me that the residents in the dining room told her what had happened to the previous resident when she revealed which apartment she had selected. This was a problem as the prior resident had committed suicide in the apartment. I could not believe the residents would be so callous to this poor woman. I had already disclosed that the preceding resident was no longer with us and that was why the apartment home was available. I obviously hadn't articulated how she died. Ultimately, after a lot of handholding, the depositor decided to go ahead and move in because it was a premium apartment. Helpful Hannahs these residents were not!

On numerous occasions, residents have walked into my office and pronounced, "I heard 'so and so' is in the hospital (or health services). Can I have their parking place (or storage locker, etc.)?" *Oh! The vultures!* I think inside my head. I calmly respond, "This is not an appropriate time to discuss this. Their parking spot (or storage locker) is theirs until we get official notification from them or their family, just as we would do with you. I will contact the first person on the waiting list when that time comes." Then I smile and wish them a great day.

There are always residents who want to come into your office and shoot the breeze, because hopefully you have built such a great relationship with them before they moved in. Give them two minutes and gently let them know that you have to prepare for an event, make a promised phone call, have a tour arriving, or are on your way to a meeting. Be consistent and do this every time they come in your office. That way you never show favoritism. Plus you get your work done. The light will click on in their brains about how busy you are. Soon they will start to say, "I know how busy you are, and I don't want to bother you, but I just want to ask you (tell you) something." Continue with allowing two minutes and then cut them off to return to your work. This is very effective and you will free up your time to get new sales.

 **Tip: Resident Council Meetings are opportunities to teach residents how to market the community to their friends.**

Most residents are trainable. They usually want to please you and be a part of the marketing efforts. A marketing director has an opportunity every month at the resident council meeting. When a marketer gives the update on occupancy, this is an opportunity to promote the next marketing event by asking residents to invite their friends. Offer a reward such as, "If you invite a friend to attend the upcoming dance performance by the university students, you may attend as well. As you know, we only have limited space in the auditorium and this event is specifically for *prospective* residents."

Maybe the next event is an open house of several apartment homes. Publicly thank those participating residents at the resident council meeting so that they have notoriety. Typically I never ask at a public meeting if anyone else would like to open up his or her apartment home. What if the pack rat resident volunteers to show his or her apartment home? Always ask *appropriate* residents *privately* if they would like to volunteer.

Take the time to have a teaching moment when speaking in front of the majority of residents. For example, teach them terminology that builds *value* with their friends and prospective residents. Make these educational moments fun and lighthearted. When residents lovingly refer to their home as a *facility*, *the home*, or *the institution*—it does *not* build value. Ask if they could please call it a "retirement community," "community," or simply "my home." Share a story such as "Before *you* moved in many of you thought that you never wanted to live in 'a facility with all those old people.'

177

(Pause for laughter here.) Some of your friends have no idea how nice the place you have chosen to live in is. Invite them to come and see your home and community!"

As residents age, their world can shrink to just within the walls of the community. Many have forgotten how a prospective resident thinks. The residents usually love their community, the staff, the dining experience, and all their fellow resident friends. Their lives are more vibrant with all the human connections instead of being isolated in their house or condo. Remind them about what is important to future residents and how they can be your ambassadors and share it with their friends.

Resident referrals usually comprise 50 percent or more of new sales. Let the residents know how valuable they are to marketing and how everyone can work together to fill the community and make new friends when new people move in. If appropriate, share how high occupancy keeps everyone's monthly fees down and thank them for being a part of the marketing team. If you treat your residents like gold (which they are!), they will be your strongest supporters.

Marketing and Administration Relationship

Everyone's definition of administration probably varies according to your organization's chart. Let's consider administration as the executive administrator, his or her assistant, the other department heads (especially human resources), and the concierges/ receptionists. It's vital to have great communication with *all* these folks and never have them be surprised, made to look ignorant, foolish, or taken off guard. It's a good idea to send a report once a week that briefly explains all upcoming marketing events. I strongly encourage you to number these and make them a consistent format. That way it's easy for administration and key staff to track.

Tip: Ask for a training session with the concierges/ receptionist/security clerk (evening shift) on exactly what to do when:

- Marketing receives a phone call
- A tour arrives
- There is an impromptu walk-in tour
- Someone walks in to just get a brochure or ask a question
- There is a marketing event

Tip: Ask the executive administrator if marketing may have an opportunity to make a presentation at an upcoming directors (department heads) meeting. This usually prompts a yes answer, but it's all about timing. Topics to discuss at a directors meeting should include:

- The vital role of *every* department making a difference to the success of marketing
- Overall marketing strategies, both on a day-to-day basis and ongoing
- The events calendar from the marketing plan, including specifically what's happening in the next quarter
- Requesting their permission to introduce prospective residents to them

- What terminology builds value for the customer and what terminology does not
- Remind them not to use the words facility, unit, or nursing home, etc.
- You might even ask each person to carry a couple of business cards with him or her

 **Tip: Find out when the next employee development (all staff) meeting will be. Ask if you may be a presenter. Potential topics:**

- Explain how each person plays a vital role to the success of marketing.
- Share how everyone is "in" the marketing department—for example, point out that a spouse was marketing (sales) when he or she asked for their hand in marriage or their significant other was marketing (sales) to them when they were asked out for a first date. (Make it fun.)
- Can they please smile and say, "Good afternoon," to guests they encounter in the hall or elevators?
- Give specific examples of how housekeeping, maintenance, and health services affect marketing in a positive way.
- Share the next upcoming marketing event.
- Thank them for being a part of the "X" number of sales or move-ins last month.

Do you respect and value your residents and co-workers?

To me, it is normal business to treat *everyone* with respect. Marketing does not work in a vacuum. We depend on residents

for referrals. Marketing relies on the environmental services (housekeeping) staff, the maintenance staff, the chef, the dining room staff, the receptionists, the administrator, the valets, the concierges, the security staff, the health services staff, the business manager, and everyone else who works in the community to contribute toward the strategic vision of 100 percent occupancy. All residents and each member of the staff at the community are a part—a vital part—of marketing.

Chapter 11
Join the Twenty-first Century with your Website, E-mail Blasts, and Social Media

You have probably seen recent headlines such as:

"Six Million More Seniors Using the Web than Five Years Ago" and "Seniors are Becoming Web-Savvy."

By the time this book is published, even more seniors will be shopping for retirement communities online. Seniors are e-mailing, surfing the web, managing digital photos, and many are even *teaching* computer classes to their peers. I believe this phenomenon began when boomers gave their parents hand-me-down computers as they upgraded to faster, newer computer models. This trend continues as some eighty-year-plus seniors are now on their second or third computer.

When surfing the web to view senior community websites, you'll find that the quality varies tremendously. The need for a well-designed website in an organization has slowly increased to a mandatory minimum standard of marketing. Yet there are many retirement community websites that have made themselves too technical and others who have embarrassingly poor content that shines a negative light back on their community.

Entire books and online articles are dedicated to making a quality website. My philosophy: It's best to hire an expert to design your website, but please remember that no one knows your organization, the marketing profession, and the prospective customer better than you. If you are not gifted as a web designer, it's up to you to manage the person or firm that is hired to create your organization's website. "Gifted" does not mean that you took a class and can do an okay job. It is vitally important to have a well-executed website.

This is how the senior customer views researching senior community websites: *The quality of your website is a direct reflection on the quality of care you provide.*

Retirement community websites fall into four categories:

The Bare Bones Website – It has your community contact information, a couple of pictures, and a couple of pages of brief information. This is almost worse than having no website. If savvy seniors are researching two communities and see one great website and a mediocre website, what will their opinion be? The seniors or their adult children may never even make the drive to tour the retirement community of the mediocre website.

Repeating the Brochure Website – Some communities give their community brochure to the web designer, and that exact information and photos are regurgitated on the website. Seniors are intelligent and pick up on this immediately. This is a lazy way to create a website. This website is typically the same one from three years ago. No new content is ever added.

Too Technical Website – These are the websites that have all the bells and whistles but forget that many seniors have older computers and cannot process them. How many websites have you visited that require you to download a program in order to view the website, watch a video testimonial, or see 360-degree views of the community? Do you download the new program? Would a senior download the program? Do you want to risk that they may not know how to download the new application to view your content? How many seniors cannot view your information and then go to your competitors' sites and become more interested in them?

The Balanced Website – It's the perfect balance of informative *current* content, *new* photography, and testimonials. It is easily managed by a nontechnical senior, piques the interest of technically savvy adult children, can be viewed by older computers, has a classy look, and creates a call to action. The website needs to be better than the competition and updated on a regular basis. (Later in this chapter I'll describe what "regular" means. When someone uses a search engine to find your community online, it should come up as the first choice—top of the page—on the search.)

185

Take Time to Research Websites

Read and view all the content of your competitors' websites. What did you like best and least? Were the colors appealing? Was the font type and size easy for seniors to read? Did they use resident models in the photography or stock photos? Do they show diversity of residents? Are there video testimonials? Did they include the floor plans and/or pricing?

Reach beyond your direct competitors to larger multi-site organizations and study their web content and approach. Do they have more pages of content? What types of photos or illustrations were enticing to the viewer? Were there social media connections such as a blog, Twitter account, Facebook account or other types?

Should floor plans and pricing be on the website?

Consider what your marketing strategies have been up to this date. You may not want to put floor plans and pricing online. Your strategy may be to give prospective guests *just enough* information to call your community. That way you can tailor the apartment style and price to their budget or home value. Many communities advocate building value for your community before disclosing the pricing. If your community has an entry fee model and chooses to put the prices online, please understand that prospective guests can often disqualify themselves. You never hear from these people because they never call. Potential customers could be slipping through your fingers and affecting occupancy.

Putting floor plans on the website can cause people to disqualify themselves as well. Adult children always want their parents in the biggest and best apartment home even though they may not be able to afford it. Adult children can view your floor plans and influence their parents to not tour your community. Please remember that the goal is to sell lifestyle and services, not real estate. It's vital that the adult children come for a visit so they *feel* how wonderful the community can be for their parent. I suggest that you mention that apartments are available in layouts of one-bedroom, one-bedroom with den, and two-bedrooms (or whatever your selection is).

How can you save money building a website?

It is rare for a marketing person to be able to design and build the community's own website. Budget is usually the issue. It can save a lot of money if you provide all the content in a page-by-page format for the designer.

Let's look at some critical information for building a balanced website:

- The main goal – To have prospective guests want to come in to tour and experience your community.
- Your brand image – Include your colors, logos, themes, key words, mission statement, font size and type, and ease of navigating the website.
- Your typical customer – The range can be from technically challenged seniors to savvy boomer children doing research for their parents.
- Photos and illustrations – This may require a new photo shoot or buying some new stock photography. Do the people look straight at you (posed) or are you capturing photos of real life and showing lifestyle. Don't forget to show diversity and equality through the website. Everyone should feel welcome. When seniors look in the mirror, they see themselves as fifteen years younger than they are. I recommend models in their early sixties to draw younger, vibrant seventy- and eighty-year-olds to tour your community.
- Resident testimonials – Try to get the best stories from your youngest looking residents. Most seniors don't want to live with "all those old people." Showing vibrancy will attract vibrancy.
- Number of pages – the more pages and content you have, the higher your placement on the search engines.
- Newsletters – A great way to add new content is by adding PDFs of your current newsletter. Some seniors will read every available back issue online if they are really interested in your community. This is usually added quarterly to semi-annually.

- Monthly calendar – Does your monthly calendar look the same as your competitors'? Try to make yours better and showcase the exciting lifestyle offered at your community. This is obviously added monthly.
- News and events – This content should be added as needed. Upcoming open houses, press releases, awards, and other pertinent information should be uploaded weekly.
- SEO - Search Engine Optimization – How do you get the big search engines to find you and rank your community online? There are many theories, but new content is always king. Create an ongoing program to add new pages, new testimonials, quarterly newsletters, current month's calendar, and updated current news and events.

Share Retirement Community Events Through an E-mail Blast

E-mail blasts are a great marketing tool to reach prospective residents, wait list members, and current residents. The postage you save could be in the thousands. It's often effective to send out a "save the date" for an event one month ahead. Give detailed information two weeks before and request RSVPs because of limited seating. Send an e-mail blast reminder four to five days before the event stating that a few spaces are still available on a first-come first-served basis.

Create a subscriber base to send an e-mail marketing blast campaign by collecting e-mail addresses from:

- Visitors to the website
- Phone inquiries to the community

- Guests who show up to tour the community
- Wait list depositors
- Residents

Tip: With an e-mail blast, you can customize your message to several groups as part of the same mailing. For example, you can send a different message to prospective guests, wait list depositors, and existing residents. You should make the title relate to the upcoming event but catchy so they will open the e-mail and view your blast. Stay away from the word "free" in your subject line or you will be lost in everyone's spam filters. It's best to just have your community name and/or the event in the subject line. Experiment and track this to determine what brings you the best results.

Please remember to adhere to all current spam laws. Always offer an option out feature if a person wants to unsubscribe. It's the law to include all your contact information such as the name, address, and phone number of your community.

Developing Green Communities with E-mail Blasts

Start-up developments typically appeal to younger seniors who are also more web savvy. Collect their e-mails and save postage by sending monthly e-mail blasts. Always offer paper copies that are mailed (snail mail). If offered a choice, future residents love saving trees (paper). It subtly shows them how you can be good stewards of the future with the way you handle operating money. Web-savvy seniors love communicating by e-mail (but remember that I always advocate for the more personal call to build relationships in answering questions). Yet an e-mail blast might be the best choice if:

- You need to get out a monthly update on construction of the new community.
- Sending a special invitation to the next retention-oriented event.
- Asking them to invite their friends to become future neighbors by coming to a lunch and learning more about the community.

E-mail blasts build trust because you are communicating with all your depositors on a regular basis. Caution: Don't rely on this technique alone. Start calling depositors that have not RSVP'd two weeks before the event. Many depositors will thank you for the call and RSVP instantly or tell you why they are unable to attend. Put all these comments in your database for future reference. Depositors who communicate with you and attend events typically move in when the building is ready for occupancy.

Senior Living and Social Media

The vibrant boomers are big on social media, so if it's not part of your current marketing plan—add it. It's about building a relationship online with current and future residents. Prospective residents learn to understand your organization by seeing how much you care for current residents and how you are willing to engage with them. This is an opportunity for you to share the lifestyle of your current residents.

You have probably heard the analogy of social media being compared to attending a dinner party. The extroverts keep the conversation upbeat, humorous, and engaging during the dinner. The introverts observe, nod, and eat. There can be cliques that break off in the kitchen and have more in-depth conversations.

If social media is new for you, it takes some time to research, get started, and patiently wait for results. I recommend shadowing someone else to determine how it will work best for your organization. It's easiest to start with one platform like Twitter or Facebook. Don't try to do it all at once and burn out. After you have mastered one platform, add a second.

Measuring Social Media Success in Senior Living

Evaluate your social media plan on a quarterly basis. Are people writing on your wall, giving you thumbs up and "like" what you're doing? It's not about quantity of friends in our social network; it's about the *quality* of those who are engaging with you. New "followers" and "friends" trickle in over time.

Some marketers' greatest frustration with social media is trying to measure a response. You hear about organizations that have one million followers and look at your community's two hundred friends and think, "what am I doing wrong?" Well, you are doing everything right when someone writes on your Facebook page about how much they appreciate what your organization did or how a specific staff member has taken great care of their parent—you can't buy that type of testimonial. Share stories that showcase your residents (with permission and only use first names) and see if residents or "friends" of your community are making comments. Keep searching for interesting topics and discussions that get a response.

Large organizations can have one person dedicated to social media. Your plan should typically include: Facebook, LinkedIn, Twitter, and a blog.

Stand-alone communities with a marketing team of what is sometimes only one person can start with one type of social media, typically Facebook. Spend a maximum of thirty to sixty minutes a day working on social media.

Some communities have engaged interns to do the social media because they understand the technical logistics and it's a way of life for them. The challenge is that they don't always understand how to put up content that will engage your prospective guest and build your brand. They need to be thoroughly trained. It is dangerous to give an intern carte blanche to your online presence and not monitor the activity.

What content do I add on social media?

- Ask engaging questions on Facebook, such as how many people do you know over seventy years old who use social media?
- Find articles through other senior resources such as LeadingAge (formerly AAHSA,) Assisted Living Federation of America (ALFA), AARP, and the Alzheimer's Association. Then repost or retweet the content you find. Look for great headlines that made *you*

open the article; it can do the same for your followers. They will have an opportunity to comment or say they like it.

The Senior Sentinel

January 5

VOL: LXXVI   **DAILY 50¢**

HEROIC POOCH SAVES SENIOR

By Oly Gunderson

HERCULES

Miss Emma Royds was saved today by her pet chihuahua Hercules. With an unbelievable feat of strength, he pulled his owner from her toilet. Miss Royd was quoted as saying "My big boy is just the best doggy-woggy in the whole world. I only feed him good healthy foods like chili con carne and popcorn." Hercules was awarded a medal and a dog bone the size of a Buick. Follow Hercules's antics on Blissful Retirement Home's blog.

marketing2seniors.net

- Look for humor or human-interest stories to share about your community.
  - o Did one of the residents' pets do something funny?
  - o Is one of your residents competing in the Senior Olympics?
  - o Your residents may have interesting family members who are involved in a current event (some examples could include, a grandson who is an astronaut, a son who has competed in

the America's Cup, or a granddaughter as a contestant for *American Idol*). Local media is always on the lookout for local connections and may retweet your headline.

- Share some real life activities that your residents are engaged in on a daily basis. Ideas might be: "Our residents enjoyed the symphony today." Maybe they saw baby snow leopards at the zoo, enjoyed some type of theater show, or visited an ostrich farm. You want your social media prospective guest to say, "Wow, I wish I lived there so I could do that too." If they say it often enough, they will come for a tour.

"I just don't have time to be responsible for social media..."

 **Tip: Spread the social media responsibility around:**

- The human resources director can be responsible for the LinkedIn account. LinkedIn is targeted toward the working professional and allows an organization to create a career profile and network for job searches.
- Have fellow employees be responsible for adding content on the Facebook or Twitter account.
  - o The health and wellness instructor can post once or twice a week. Topics might include: "Eighteen residents felt relaxed and rejuvenated after yoga (tai chi) class today" or "How long will it take our residents to exercise their way to Oregon (or your next state)?"
  - o The activities or resident services director can post once or twice a week. Topics might include: performances (especially

in the evening when people can't drive in the dark), painting or art exhibits, and resident outings.

o The dining director should post once a week or every two weeks, sharing the dinner entrée selections or details about a themed dinner such as Oktoberfest.

o Is there a Paparazzi Pat who can upload videos to YouTube and then post the link on your Facebook account?

o If any of the people above do not excel in the written word, they can give the content ideas to the marketer to post online.

o This leaves the marketer to add articles and interesting content from other senior resources. You can also publicize your upcoming events such as: "Our open house event is happening on Wednesday. (Link to info on your web page.) Are you coming?"

Ultimately it's important to have and keep current content on:

1. **A well-designed website that's easy to read and navigate.**
2. **E-mail blasts sent to announce upcoming marketing events.**
3. **Social media such as Facebook, Twitter, YouTube, and LinkedIn to engage and connect with your residents and prospective guests with real time events.**

Chapter 12
Media Buying,
Public Relations, and
Community Relations
with a Skinny Piggy Bank

If your occupancy needs immediate improvement, media buying can get your message out there fast. The downside is that it comes with a high price tag. Most people ask me, "How do I increase the occupancy without breaking the bank (or for the lowest cost)?" Without knowing your specific situation and competitors, I will give you sound general principles in this chapter that really work.

From Wikipedia, the free encyclopedia:

"Media Buying" is a sub function of advertising management. Media Buying is the procurement of the best possible placement and price of a piece of media real-estate within any given media. The main task of Media Buying lies within the negotiation of price and placement to ensure the best possible value can be secured.

Retirement communities will select different types of media based on their desire to create a national or local presence.

Traditional media includes:
- Newspapers
  - o City/town dailies
  - o Community/neighborhood weeklies
  - o Smaller publications targeted toward seniors
- Radio (select stations that attract seniors)
- TV (programs that have a high percentage of senior viewers such as the news)
- Magazines (look for a high readership of seniors)

Newer media choices include:
- Internet (Tip: Your web designer may be able to share helpful information about advertising online.)
  - o E-mails/E-mail blasts
  - o Search engines and referral links
  - o Web portals
  - o Web banners
- Premium cable or satellite TV
- Satellite radio

Advertising choices include:
- Direct mail pieces
- Newsletters

First, before you spend any money on media and advertising, is your community ready for the phone to ring off the hook? Will every call be answered in two to four rings? What is the first impression in the parking lot, your main entrance, and at the front desk reception area? If your evaluation is positive, then let's create an event to attract the prospective resident. Please read the chapter "Great Events Can Fill Your Building" before proceeding to the next step.

Secondly, has your brand image been established? Do you have a logo, colors, and a look that the prospective resident recognizes? Do all your collateral pieces have a themed look? In other words, does your brochure, website, signage outside your community, direct mail pieces, newsletters, and newspapers ads have a brand identity? Please refer to the branding chapter in this book "Dare to Differentiate Yourself from Your Competition" for more information.

Third, are you going to make the media choices in-house with your marketing director or hire an advertising agency? What are the media choices in your town or city? You may say, "How hard is it to run an ad in the local paper?" That ad is going to represent your community and if someone inexperienced in media selection makes an unfortunate choice, people may now view your health care as unsuitable for themselves or their parents. Choose wisely... it's very possible to train an inexperienced marketing director, but it takes time.

Strategies to Media Buying and Advertising

You already know that your target audiences are seniors who need to be age and income qualified and adult children who can influence their parents' decisions. The goal has already been determined to increase occupancy by having more prospective guests walk through your front door to experience your community.

The value of advertising can be determined by the cost per thousand and then the number of new leads it generates for you. Television uses the Nielsen ratings to determine cost per thousand, and newspapers base theirs on the circulation. Obviously someone can have the TV on and not be watching it or subscribe to the newspaper and leave it unread or not read the page where your ad appears.

The Big Three Traditional Media Choices:

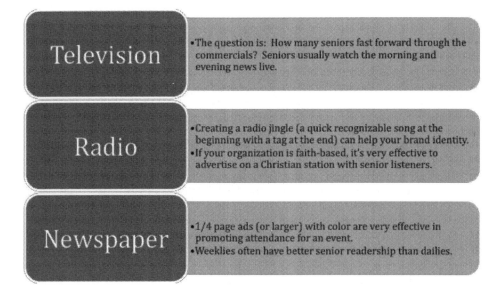

Television	•The question is: How many seniors fast forward through the commercials? Seniors usually watch the morning and evening news live.
Radio	•Creating a radio jingle (a quick recognizable song at the beginning with a tag at the end) can help your brand identity. •If your organization is faith-based, it's very effective to advertise on a Christian station with senior listeners.
Newspaper	•1/4 page ads (or larger) with color are very effective in promoting attendance for an event. •Weeklies often have better senior readership than dailies.

Television can take the biggest bite out of your budget. It also involves the creation of fifteen to sixty seconds of quality video with your branding message and event interweaved. This is a good medium to build your brand and exposure to become a household name.

Radio stations will share their demographics strengths with you. Don't waste your budget on popular radio stations attracting only young people. Concentrate on National Public Radio (NPR), talk radio, classical, and jazz stations. If a station has a political agenda, consider if you want your community to be associated or labeled as a supporter. Even if the politics coincide with your own beliefs, understand that prospective residents come from a variety of political affiliations. Radio buys can be expensive but effective in driving customers to events and building brand awareness of your community.

Newspapers and senior publications can be extremely effective in advertising an event to seniors. Always check the cost per thousand and whether it's a paid subscription or a free publication. If it's free, where is it distributed? Are the age and income qualified seniors going to pick up a free copy from those locations? You can request a certain placement of your ad in the paper. Print media can't always deliver on a promise, but they strive to meet your placement request. Ads always cost more on the back page of a section. People read from left to right and from top to bottom. Section A usually has good senior readership but costs more. The crossword puzzle page is often less expensive and seniors usually see that page.

Magazines have very specific audiences. These tend to be utilized in national campaigns with multiple retirement communities.

Tip: What gives the most bang for the buck in advertising retirement communities? The answer is direct mail.

Keeping the costs affordable in the marketing plan

Senior housing for-profits have larger advertising budgets than non-profits. It's important to allocate the proper amount of advertising money in order to generate enough new leads to increase occupancy. It can be as simple as the CFO report described in chapter one to request additional funds from management. How much should you request? Each situation is unique. Sometimes an outside marketing specialist is needed to evaluate the appropriate amount of resources based on your particular market and competition. This could be money well spent if an effective plan based on your budget is developed to fill your community. I would be happy to discuss this with you.

The media buys and advertising in the marketing plan need to address both short- and long-term marketing goals. Cost-effective choices for retirement communities on a tight budget are:

- Direct mail pieces – can build long-term brand awareness of your community to the target audience (a purchased list that is age and income qualified) by inviting participation at upcoming events with a call to action (short-term). Invitation examples could be to attend "lunch and learns" or major events.
- Quarterly (or semi-annual) newsletters – showcase the ongoing lifestyle of your residents though pictures, articles, and testimonials. The short-term benefits are immediate calls, but this medium is also very effective for creating long-term interest in your community.
- E-mail blasts – target your existing database to attend an event.
- Newspaper ads – drive new attendance to a particular event.

The magic three to build attendance at an event

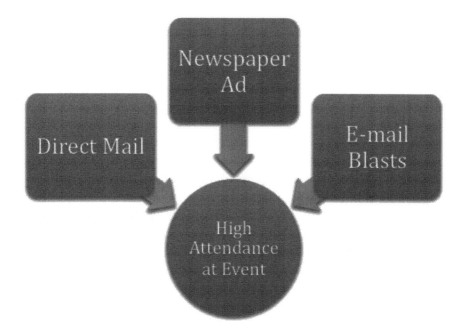

The above magic three should produce the following magic three:

- **One-third new prospective guests**
- **One-third wait list**
- **One-third taking a second look at your community**

Public Relations

Public relations is like free advertising. It could be considered good press or bad depending on the angle of the article. Build relationships with your local reporters.

Tip: If you have a newspaper budget for events, ask local publications to feature your community in an upcoming article to run adjacent to an ad of your retirement community inviting guests to an event. They may ask you to write the article. Smaller weeklies are very receptive to these types of ideas. I recommend hiring an affordable public relations consultant—not a firm, which can be very expensive. I know a wonderful, affordable ghostwriter who has written award-winning articles with my byline: www.marketing2seniors.net

Press releases

Press releases can be sent by e-mail, but relationships with reporters can make a difference. Typically press releases are sent to thirty or more different sources. They are sent to newspapers, TV, radio, and senior publications. Many papers have complimentary event listings (especially for senior-oriented events), and with proper notification your announcement can be listed for free. Often they have extremely early deadlines (holiday publications may require listings three months in advance), so get them the information as quickly as possible—months out. Don't be sales-y in these. Just give the straight facts of who, what, where, and when. Radio stations may give your event a quick plug, especially if you run some radio spots too.

Newspapers are looking for content on low news days. When I let the press know a horse was going to visit the local skilled nursing center, there was no response from them. After the event, I supplied them with a photo of a hundred-year-old resident hugging the head of the horse. The photo landed on the front page and included a short, heart-warming article on our community. Persistence and timing can pay off.

 **Tip: Small newspapers usually cannot afford to send a photographer but will often publish a photo you send to them. Make sure to include a caption and credit who took the photo.**

Having any old performance at your community is not newsworthy. Having a "Mayoral Debate" can bring the press (there is no political favoritism if both sides are present). When I organized a live Nativity, I received free promos on the local Christian radio station, a complimentary listing of the event in the daily newspaper, and had a front-page article in the weekly newspaper after the event. The newspaper wanted to publicize the intergenerational volunteer involvement: The senior residents built the manger and stable structure in the woodshop. Heaters were required in the winter to entice a young mother to volunteer her baby to be Jesus. The animals were the easiest to obtain but required a lot of logistics, and a local high school drama group received extra credit for portraying Mary, Joseph, the shepherds, and the wise men.

Community Relations

What are you doing to help your fellow man? Prospective guests, neighbor influencers, and local businesses like to see this...it builds trust that your organization cares.

The local neighborhood residents and business owners have an opinion of your retirement community. It's often the wrong one. It's normal for them to give you old generic names like a facility for old people, a nursing home, or an assisted living place. Your community may be a young and vibrant continuing care retirement community or an independent community but have the wrong labels with the locals.

How do you transpose "old" labels?

It's a matter of leaving your campus to reach out and touch influential neighbors and businesses. Always have an example to share of how your vibrant residents are reaching out to help neighbors in need. Maybe your community can host a blood drive or food drive. What if upon moving in your residents donated their extra furniture to a charity that helps low-income families reestablish themselves in a residence? What about building a foundation for residents who outlive their resources?

 **Tip: Ask your present and prospective residents where they currently volunteer. If one or two opportunities appeal to your organization, maybe staff can be encouraged to volunteer or your bus can bring more residents at one time to volunteer.**

These are some of the good connections to make:

- Chamber of commerce
- Rotary
- Colleges and universities
- Hospitals
- Downtown associations
- Meet the Mayor
- Connect with your city council
- Have your community participate in the local parade
- Local business events
- Don't forget the competition

Your organization represents seniors and employment in the neighborhood. This is a powerful combination that few take lightly. Many types of businesses would love to have access to your residents. Others organizations can be asking your company for donations on a regular basis. Protecting residents and managing the budget allocations are vital. Consider what is mutually beneficial. Universities asking for money can be very satisfied presenting a lifelong learning seminar or having their drama or opera students perform for the residents.

Politics and Causes?

Getting involved in a political issue can be a bit tricky. Always receive the blessing of your boss and/or the CEO to make sure it's a cause that benefits the residents. Politics are almost always time drains, so beware. I became very involved in protecting views for a community as the city was rezoning heights. The CEO, the administrator, and almost every resident became involved in writing influential letters that made a difference to the outcome. Sometimes it's easier to let others do the quibbling and write a letter representing the community at a strategic time of public influence.

Tip: Some of the greatest tours you can give are to the mayor, city council members, local CEOs, and other powerful influencers in your neighborhood or city. Always offer them a lunch with the tour and don't forget to send thank you notes. These influencers go out and tell other people about the positive attributes of your community. Don't forget to take pictures with their permission and include their visit in your next newsletter. This is how you build a great public image and break the labels of "an old nursing home" or "that assisted living place."

Reach out to connect with prospective guests, influential people, and businesses within an eight-mile radius through advertising and the media. Be budget and time conscious. Marketing directors need to use their time strategically. If you join a chamber of commerce, it is not necessary to attend *every* meeting, but you should be there several times throughout the year. The attendance of potential residents at an event will determine the success of advertising dollars spent. Community relations can be analyzed on a yearly basis to determine which memberships had the most impact on influencing your brand image within an eight-mile radius to indirectly increase occupancy.

Some of These Keys not Fitting Your Doors?

My sincere hope is that this book has added the appropriate keys to your keychain to unlock any doors blocking your marketing success.

Some industry professionals believe that if you give away secrets of marketing success, then the competition will use them against you. That is not my philosophy. The 12 keys that I chose to share unlock the doors of the "rooms" where I have observed and experienced organizations struggling most often.

Quality marketing people are always needed who can relentlessly make follow-up calls to new inquiries and especially follow up after tours. Even then, they are not done. They have to be able to master discovering the needs, personality, objections, and hot buttons of every prospective resident. With all that information in play, it is literally "art in action" to influence someone to make a decision, close the sale, and have them choose to move in as soon as possible. If anyone could do it, then marketing people would be paid minimum wage. Right?

If your occupancy is high, please appreciate the dedication, constant rejection, and hard work of your marketing team. Celebrate and reward their success—today!

Maybe your occupancy is down and you need your financial performance to improve immediately. It's faster to train your current marketing team than hire a brand new one.

Examine Your Sales Mentoring and Coaching

- Is your sales team unwittingly sabotaging their sales?
- Are they answering *every* inbound call within two rings and greeting walk-in appointments within five minutes?
- Are they over-sharing information with the prospective resident?
- Do they fail to identify closing questions?
- Could your marketing team benefit from some sales training from an outside senior marketing specialist to improve their techniques? Scheduling appointments? Effective follow ups? Closing sales?

Re-visit Your Marketing Plan, Strategies, and Media Mix

- Do you need an outside senior marketing specialist to create an effective marketing plan for your unique market conditions?
- Should a new set of eyes evaluate your SWOT—strengths, weaknesses, opportunities, and threats?
- Are you confident that you are using the right media mix to generate the most leads with your budget?

Are You Conducting *Ongoing* Analysis of Your Competition, Pricing, Branding, and Incentives?

- Is the competition stealing all or some of your sales?
- Does a fresh strategy need to be developed by an outside senior marketing specialist in order to compete more effectively?
- Is your pricing competitive? Does it need analysis?

Some of These Keys not Fitting Your Doors?

- Is your brand unrecognized or poorly perceived? Does it need revamping?
- Are your incentives motivating customers to sell their homes *now*?

You have a choice to either have a targeted plan of action to increase occupancy or just throw more money at it...

Marketing 2 Seniors is dedicated to helping stand-alone and multi-site senior living communities increase their occupancy—and stay full. To show that I really mean that, help is just an e-mail away.

If you are an association, I will donate some books when speaking to your organization.

For more information:
Web: www.marketing2seniors.net
E-mail: diane@marketing2seniors.net
Twitter: @market2seniors

About the Author:

Diane Twohy Masson is an award-winning certified aging services professional (CASP) with a B.S. in business management and a minor in marketing from Central Washington University. She has also earned advanced social media certification. Masson has worked in senior housing marketing since 1999, after helping her mother find a retirement community. Masson's management expertise, strategies, and sales team coaching have been instrumental in marketing existing continuing care retirement communities (CCRCs), assisted living communities, and developing brand new urban CCRCs in Washington, Oregon, and California.

Masson develops strategies to keep sales volume high, creates brands that become household names with seniors, and orchestrates the right media marketing mix to bring customers to the door, but understands it takes more than that. Existing retirement communities have increased from 90 percent to 100 percent occupancy in just over a year under Masson's leadership. During a tough economic time, her marketing strategies with a brand new CCRC led to 185 apartment home move-ins within eighteen months.

She enjoys public speaking, golfing, traveling, bird watching, writing, hiking, camping, reading, scripture study, and spending time with her family.

Made in the USA
Lexington, KY
17 October 2012